Rock Climbs of Tuolumne Meadows

Rock Climbs of Tuolumne Meadows

Third Edition

Don Reid and Chris Falkenstein

Chockstone Press
Evergreen, Colorado
1992

_2627, 1992_

GV
149.42
.c22
TL866
1992

CMC

Rock Climbs of Tuolumne Meadows – 3rd Edition

All photos by Chris Falkenstein

Cover photo: Tom Herbert on Rising Sun, 5.13c, Pywiack Dome

ISBN 0-934641-47-1

Published and Distributed by
Chockstone Press, Inc.
Post Office Box 3505
Evergreen, CO 80439

ACKNOWLEDGEMENTS

WE WOULD LIKE TO THANK the following people, for without their help and support this guide would not have been possible: Steve Schneider for sharing his vast knowledge of Medlicott Dome and the Twin Bridges Area; Errett Allen for his help with the Twin Bridges Area; Michael Forkash for his overall awareness of the area; Carolly Hauksdottir for her fine art work; Dan McDevitt, Tom Herbert, Dave Bengston, Urmas Franosch, Bruce Morris, Alan Nelson, Ken Yager, Grant Hiskes; and to anyone else that we may have forgotten. Thanks!!!

WARNING: CLIMBING IS A SPORT WHERE YOU MAY BE SERIOUSLY INJURED OR DIE.
READ THIS BEFORE YOU USE THIS BOOK.

This guidebook is a compilation of unverified information gathered from many different climbers. The author cannot assure the accuracy of any of the information in this book, including the topos and route descriptions, the difficulty ratings, and the protection ratings. These may be incorrect or misleading and it is impossible for any one author to climb all the routes to confirm the information about each route. Also, ratings of climbing difficulty and danger are always subjective and depend on the physical characteristics (for example, height), experience, technical ability, confidence and physical fitness of the climber who supplied the rating. Additionally, climbers who achieve first ascents sometimes underrate the difficulty or danger of the climbing route out of fear of being ridiculed if a climb is later down-rated by subsequent ascents. Therefore, be warned that you must exercise your own judgment on where a climbing route goes, its difficulty and your ability to safely protect yourself from the risks of rock climbing. Examples of some of these risks are: falling due to technical difficulty or due to natural hazards such as holds breaking, falling rock, climbing equipment dropped by other climbers, hazards of weather and lightning, your own equipment failure, and failure of fixed protection.

You should not depend on any information gleaned from this book for your personal safety; your safety depends on your own good judgment, based on experience and a realistic assessment of your climbing ability. If you have any doubt as to your ability to safely climb a route described in this book, do not attempt it.

The following are some ways to make your use of this book safer:

1. **CONSULTATION:** You should consult with other climbers about the difficulty and danger of a particular climb prior to attempting it. Most local climbers are glad to give advice on routes in their area and we suggest that you contact locals to confirm ratings and safety of particular routes and to obtain first-hand information about a route chosen from this book.

2. **INSTRUCTION:** Most climbing areas have local climbing instructors and guides available. We recommend that you engage an instructor or guide to learn safety techniques and to become familiar with the routes and hazards of the areas described in this book. Even after you are proficient in climbing safely, occasional use of a guide is a safe way to raise your climbing standard and learn advanced techniques.

3. **FIXED PROTECTION:** Many of the routes in this book use bolts and pitons which are permanently placed in the rock. Because of variances in the manner of placement, weathering, metal fatigue, the quality of the metal used, and many other factors, these fixed protection pieces should always be considered suspect and should always be backed up by equipment that you place yourself. Never depend for your safety on a single piece of fixed protection because you never can tell whether it will hold weight.

Be aware of the following specific potential hazards which could arise in using this book:

1. **MISDESCRIPTIONS OF ROUTES:** If you climb a route and you have a doubt as to where the route may go, you should not go on unless you are sure that you can go that way safely. Route descriptions and topos in this book may be inaccurate or misleading.

2. **INCORRECT DIFFICULTY RATING:** A route may, in fact be more difficult than the rating indicates. Do not be lulled into a false sense of security by the difficulty rating.

3. **INCORRECT PROTECTION RATING:** If you climb a route and you are unable to arrange adequate protection from the risk of falling through the use of fixed pitons or bolts and by placing your own protection devices, do not assume that there is adequate protection available higher just because the route protection rating indicates the route is not an "X" or an "R" rating. Every route is potentially an "X" (a fall may be deadly), due to the inherent hazards of climbing, including, for example, failure of fixed protection, your own equipment's failure, or improper use of climbing equipment.

THERE ARE NO WARRANTIES, WHETHER EXPRESS OR IMPLIED, THAT THIS GUIDEBOOK IS ACCURATE OR THAT THE INFORMATION CONTAINED IN IT IS RELIABLE. THERE ARE NO WARRANTIES OF FITNESS FOR A PARTICULAR PURPOSE OR THAT THIS GUIDE IS MERCHANTABLE. YOUR USE OF THIS BOOK INDICATES YOUR ASSUMPTION OF THE RISK THAT IT MAY CONTAIN ERRORS AND IS AN ACKNOWLEDGEMENT OF YOUR OWN SOLE RESPONSIBILITY FOR YOUR CLIMBING SAFETY.

CONTENTS

INTRODUCTION

CLEAN ROCK, CLEAR SKIES AND AN AIRY high-country atmosphere – this is Tuolumne. This book describes the rock climbing routes in a region of classically rounded, granitic domes within Yosemite National Park in California. The majority of these domes and cliffs overlook a seven-mile stretch of road leading into Tuolumne Meadows, the largest alpine meadow of the Sierra Nevada. Referred to as "Tuolumne" or "The Meadows" by climbers, this area is sixty miles from Yosemite Valley (perhaps a quarter of that distance as the crow flies). At 8,500 feet, it is pristine and beautiful, often uncrowded and always cool in summer. It also offers the rock climber excellent face and crack climbing on sound white and orange granite, as well as excellent alpine rock climbs on some of the surrounding high peaks.

California Highway 120, the main access route to Tuolumne, runs east from the town of Manteca, climbs up past the mouth of Yosemite Valley, through The Meadows, over Tioga Pass and on to Lee Vining, a small town on the east side of the Sierra. Depending on snowfall, which can vary widely from year to year, the road is open to The Meadows from late May through late fall. In the winter, the road is open only to ski travel. A $5 one-week car pass or a $15 annual Yosemite Pass is assessed for each vehicle entering Yosemite National Park. A $25 Golden Eagle Pass allows unlimited travel into all the National Parks.

SERVICES

Limited bus service is offered during the summer months from Yosemite Valley into Tuolumne Meadows, across Tioga Pass to Lee Vining, and back again. A vehicle is almost essential to get to the climbs of Tuolumne, since hitchhiking can sometimes be difficult.

A small store, cafe (grill), gas station and climbing school are located in The Meadows. A large campground also is found here. Campsites are offered on a first-come, first-served basis, but the campground is rarely full – except on weekends and holidays. The current daily cost per site is $10, with a six-person maximum. A 14-day camping limit is enforced. Smaller campgrounds are available both east and west of The Meadows.

You should take several precautions when camping near Tuolumne. Keeping food from the sometimes persistent bears is the primary concern. All food should be locked out of sight in a vehicle or suspended between trees, out of reach of tree-climbing bears. Of similar concern is human thievery. Although not as common-place as in Yosemite Valley, take care when storing valuables.

Tuolumne Meadows Lodge is one mile east of the main campground. Rooms, showers and meals can be purchased here. a laundromat, bars, cafes and cheaper food can be found just twenty miles east over Tioga Pass in Lee Vining.

In case of emergency, call 911, or the Park Service Dispatcher at 372-0214. The nearest hospital is either in Yosemite Valley (60 miles) or Mammoth Lakes (40 miles), on the east side of the Sierra.

CLIMATE

The best months for climbing in Tuolumne are June, July and August, when temperatures average 30°-50° at night and 65°-75° during the day. Most of the precipitation in The Meadows occurs during the winter, and long dry spells are common in the summer months. These can be interrupted by an occasional snowstorm, but midafternoon thunderstorms can develop. These storms can be quite violent, with much hail and lightning, before the sky clears at evening. When a weather pattern of afternoon thunderstorms predominates, it is wise to select climbs that preclude being caught anywhere high or exposed when the rains come. Climbing accidents in Tuolumne are rare, but most have occurred in conjunction with the "surprise" afternoon thunderstorm.

GEOLOGY

The Tuolumne Meadows region contains eleven major domes with several smaller satellite humps, all scattered along a broad, rolling valley.

The Meadows area is part of the Sierra Batholith, a huge mass of crystalline, igneous rock that extends into the earth to great depths and was formed about 210 million years ago. Approximately 100 million years ago, the batholith was brought to the surface through uplift and erosion.

The granite rock of the Tuolumne area, specifically granite porphyrite, is very hard but prone to exfoliation, which has created the characteristic dome shape. Granite porphyrite is made up chiefly of quartz, feldspar and mica. About three million years ago, the Tuolumne domes were subjected to at least three periods of glaciation, further shaping them and producing the glacier polish that is still abundant throughout the area.

THE CLIMBING

Seas of knobs, ⅛-inch edges and sharp angular crystals characterize the exquisite face climbing on the domes and rocks in the Tuolumne Meadows area. While the majority of the climbing is on featured faces, the interesting cracks will keep even the hardcore crack enthusiast busy for some time.

The rock in Tuolumne is usually solid (except for the occasional loose flake) extremely clean and, when available, cracks offer solid protection. As one might expect, bolts are the main form of protection on the face routes. The majority are the old ¼-inch by 2-inch Rawl type. Some have been in place for at least ten years, and one should exercise caution and use common sense when these older bolts are used.

Long runouts exist on most of the face climbs and this is particularly true on the easier routes, as they were probably put up by better climbers. Be prepared for runouts of 40 to 60 feet on hard climbs, with little to no pro on the easier (5.8 range) pitches. Climbs known for notoriously long runouts include **The Kid, You**

Asked For It, and the all-time classic pucker test piece, the **Bachar-Yerian.** Keep in ming that bolts are hard to find on the wide open faces, as they may resemble a knob or stain on the rock.

Be forewarned that many climbs here were done in a style offering little or no protection, with serious if not fatal consequences arising if one were to fall. Tuolumne probably is not a good place to learn to climb (except, of course, for the crack climbs), for if you are in the middle of a blank face and freak out because of no pro, there is not much you can do! This guide simply tells where the climbs are and gives a subjective rating of the expected moves. The user of this book is expected to judge the protection situation as it unfolds ahead of them.

Luckily, common sense and the idea that climbing can be an enjoyably safe adventure are starting to take hold here. Almost every new climb established since 1988 has adequate protection, using the new, two- to three-inch long Rawl five-piece bolts in either the ⅜-inch or ½-inch diameter. Much needed retro-bolting also is taking place, with anchors and lead protection being replaced on some of the more popular climbs.

Many of the newer climbs follow lines up the prominent black streaks that are seen on the domes. Running water has eroded the granite, leaving the more weather-resistant feldspar crystals. Classic examples of these black streak climbs are **Shadow of Doubt, Bachar-Yerian, Knobvious,** and **Love Sexy.** Sport climbs have also gained popularity, offering great pro, usually a short pitch, and easy lower-offs.

EQUIPMENT

The climbing gear needed for the Tuolumne routes will depend on the type of climb. The standard rack for a face climb includes some smaller Friends, T.C.U.s, a good selection of R.P.s or similar micro nuts, some special 5⁄16-inch slings (for knob tieoffs), many quickdraws and numerous free carabiners. Crack climbs may require a rack consisting of many Friends (or Hexcentrics), R.P.s and stoppers ranging in size from ¼-inch to 4 inches. Some routes require many nuts of similar size due to the unvarying nature of the crack. **Handbook, Arch Rival** and **Speed of Life** are typical of such routes.

Bolts are utilized extensively on face climbs and for many belays. Most common are ¼-inch diameter Rawl Drives in either a 1¼-inch or 2¼-inch length. Caution and common sense should be exercised when clipping into bolts, because constant exposure to avalanches and freezing and thawing within the bolt hole has a weakening effect. Please leave all hangers and bolts in place and DO NOT hit with a hammer, as this will cause damage to the bolt and its placement.

Fixed pitons are found on many routes and should be tested with a hammer or used with great care. They often loosen over the years for lack of adequate and violent testing. Leave all existing pitons in place and avoid adding them to existing routes.

Most routes have either a sling belay or small stance; therefore, one should use a good harness or belay seat.

LOCAL ETHICS AND CUSTOMS

As we all know, climbing ethics have become a very debatable subject as of late. It seems that everyone has his or her own view of how climbing should be undertaken. The purest ascent would be done in barefooted and with no rope or equipment of any kind. Of course, few climb like this, so maybe a happy medium can be reached.

Ninety-nine percent of the climbs in Tuolumne go free, which means they have been led without the climber resorting to resting or hanging on the gear. Most of the first-ascent parties used traditional methods, but depending on who you talk to, traditional has different meanings. Some may have resorted to previewing, sieging, yo-yoing, or even using a hook or piton to drill pro off of. And, yes, even rap-bolting is done here. These routes may have been toproped and pre-protected before being led through.

Whatever the technique used by the first-ascent party, this should not deter one from sampling the fine climbs that Tuolumne has to offer. The bottom line here is the final product, one to be enjoyed and savored like a fine wine.

When climbing here one may observe different styles being utilized: A person going for the flash; some beginners pulling on their pro to get past a hard spot; a party hang-dogging. Whatever the style, please respect the choice, and maybe we won't have any more parking-lot wars.

Camping here is a little bit more relaxed than in the Yosemite Valley Police State. Just follow the simple rules and you can avoid the sometimes overzealous rangers. If you plan to bandit camp or if you try to sleep in the back of a camper, you will probably get busted. Camping out of the park – a 10-minute drive east – is somewhat mellower and camping in your car is virtually hassle-free.

An escape from Tuolumne to the east side can be a pleasant diversion. The Deadmans climbing/bouldering areas are just 45 minutes east and then south down Highway 395 towards Mammoth Lakes. Steep, overhanging, pocketed volcanic rock, with great topropes and some short leads, are found here. Another hour's travel south on Highway 395 will bring you to the Owens River Gorge, which is just north of Bishop.

As we all know, climbing has soared in popularity, creating a visual and environmental impact that we should all be aware of. To help preserve the quality of climbing now found in Tuolumne for ourselves and future generations please:

• Pack out all trash, such as cigarette butts, tape, beer cans, slings, etc.

• Don't chisel, scar, or glue on holds. Leave the rock as you found it.

• Use rock-colored bolt hangers instead of colored ones.

• Try not to leave bright-colored back-off slings and try to clean off old ones.

• Help keep the Park Service off climbers' backs by leaving areas cleaner than you found them. Help educate others.

• It is against the law to use motorized drills.

Ratings

The Yosemite Decimal System is used throughout this guide. Developed at Tahquitz Rock, in southern California, this is now the accepted American grading system. The system is "open ended," and rising standards result in more grades.

An a, b, c, or d suffix is often added to the higher grades to further define the difficulty. The following is a rough comparison of the major rating systems in use in the world today:

West German	YDS	British	Australian	East German	French
	5.0				
	5.1				
	5.2				
	5.3				
	5.4				
	5.5				
	5.6				
5+	5.7	4b / VS		VIIa	5a
6-	5.8	4c / VS	15	VIIb	5b
6	5.9	5a / HVS	16 / 17	VIIb	5c
6+	5.10a		18	VIIc	6a
7-	5.10b	5b / E1	19	VIIIa	6a+
7	5.10c	E2	20	VIIIb	6b
7+	5.10d		21	VIIIc	6b+
	5.11a	5c		IXa	6c
8-	5.11b	E3	22		6c
8	5.11c		23	IXb	6c+
8+	5.11d	6a	24	IXc	7a
9-	5.12a	E4	25	Xa	7a+
9	5.12b		26	Xb	7b
	5.12c	6b / E5	27		7b+
9+	5.12d		28	Xc	7c
10-	5.13a	6c			7c+
10	5.13b	E6	29		8a
	5.13c	7a	30		8a+
10+	5.13d	E7	31		8b
11-	5.14a		32		8b+

After the name and rating of each climb, one will also find the following to help in better understanding the quality of the climb and the abundance or lack of protection:

★   above average quality

★★   very high quality

★★★   extremely excellent climb; must do

?   unknown quality

PG   a climb with excellent protection, bolts or crack

R   a climb with serious runouts

X   extremely long runouts with possible fatal consequences if one falls

?   unknown protection

USE OF THIS GUIDE

California Highway 120 is used as the major reference line for the routes and domes of this guide. The topos and written descriptions start with the routes on the northern side of Hwy. 120 at the western end of the climbing area. They then follow the routes east into Tuolumne Meadows, staying on the north side of the road. A chapter follows that includes a section of better routes on the surrounding higher mountains. Then, the remainder of the route descriptions follow west along the south side of Hwy.120 to Tenaya Lake and Dike Dome. The maps located on page 8, 9, and 11 will help the reader locate the rock formations hidden in the woods. Additionally, photos sit amid the descriptions. Finally, at the end of the book is an index of bolt-protected sport climbs, an index of routes by their rating, route and page index.

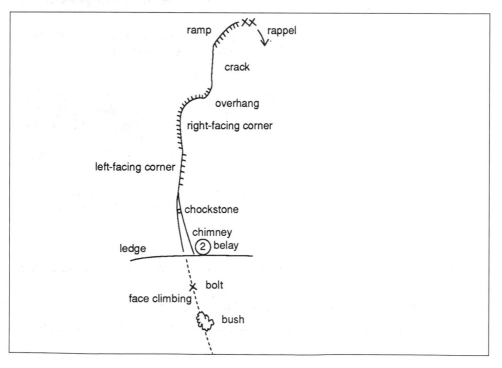

EASY SET UP — FUN TOP ROPES

If you are looking for an escape one day, from that daily grind of putting your butt on the line leading or you just want a mega workout, here is a list of existing top ropes and also climbs that are easily top roped.

Murphy Creek Many different sized cracks, several with bolt anchors on top, are found here. Page 20.

Black Angel 5.11a Set up with small to medium sized friends, 80 feet. Page 21.

Death Crack 5.11d 2 bolts, 95 feet. Page 21.

Chinese Handcuffs 5.10d Friends, T.C.U.'s, 80 feet. Page 29.

Guppie Wall 90-foot face climbs in the 5.10 range with tree and bolt anchors. Approach from the right side. Page 32.

Scruffy Underbelly 5.11c Located on the small orange and black cliff left of the lower part of Mountaineer's Dome, T.C.U.'s and friends, 40 feet. Page 34.

Laser Blade 5.12c Bring 1½ , 2, 2½, friends to get down to the 2-bolt anchor, 60 feet. Page 42.

Quick Release 5.12a Little bit scary getting down to the 2-bolt anchor, 50 feet. Page 42.

Love Supreme 5.13b Bring small friends, T.C.U.'s, and wired's, 60 feet. Page 42.

Memo From Loyd 5.10d Finger and hand crack, approach on ledge from its right side, 2 bolts, 50 feet. Page 44.

Galen's Crack 5.10c Fist-offwidth, located on the north side of the road (Hwy. 120) across from the Yawn on Medlicott Dome. 30 feet, 3+4 friends. Page 40.

Falkenstein Face 5.10+ Face just right of Galen's Crack.

South Whiz Dome A multitude of high quality knob climbs from 5.10 to 5.13. **Blackout, Count Down** and **Shockwave**, will require two 165-foot ropes, off their 2-bolt anchors. **Shadow Warrior, Super Sonic, Love Sexy,** and **Fame and Fortune** require a short rappel off of bolts so you can get down to their respective 2-bolt anchors and then one rope, doubled (80 feet), is used. Page 45.

Skeletor 5.11d; **Rap It Up** 5.12d; and **Wild Streak** 5.12a These knob climbs are located on Hammer Dome. Rappel off bolts down steep slabs to reach the anchor bolts. 80 feet. Page 48.

River Wall Most of these routes can be tried off of bolts. Page 49.

Western Front Several of these climbs can be tried from 2-bolt anchors on the top of the ridge, 80 feet. Page 54.

Peanut Gallery Almost all off of bolts, 80 feet. Pages 61-2.

Canopy World Most of the climbs can be easily top-roped off bolts, 80 feet. Page 65.

Pot Luck 5.11a 30-foot; Friends. Page 91.

Puppy Dome The climbs **Dor Or Fly** 5.11c and **Grenade Launcher** 5.12c are easily top roped off of bolt anchors, 80 feet. Page 89.

Cruise Control 5.12d Located 50 feet right of the first pitch of **Little Sheba** on Lamb Dome, approach from the right side, rappel off little pine tree to the 2-bolt anchor, 80 feet. Page 110.

Groundeffects 5.11c Rappel off same pine tree as for Cruise Control to the 2 bolts, 80 feet. Page 110.

Manu Wall (back side of Pywiack Dome) The climbs **Rising Sun** 5.13c; **Electric Africa** 5.12d; **Clash of the Titans** 5.13b; and **European Vacation** 5.13b can be top roped off of bolts. Approach up easy chimney left of **Electric Africa** to a small pine tree and then rappel off one large bolt to 2-bolt anchors at the top of the climbs, 80 feet. Page 141.

Guns of Navarone This thirty-foot wall offers a multitude of fun top ropes in the 5.10 to 5.12 range. Cracks and face are top roped off bolts at the top. Page 150.

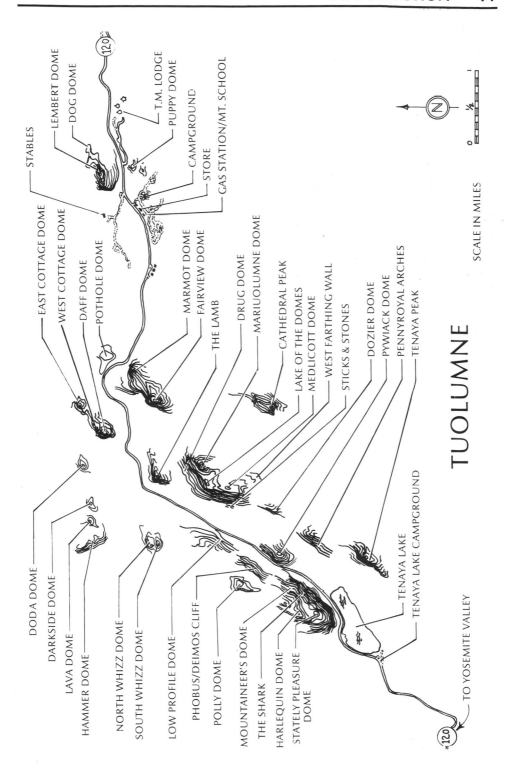

STABLES
LEMBERT DOME
DOG DOME
T.M. LODGE
PUPPY DOME
CAMPGROUND
STORE
GAS STATION/MT. SCHOOL

EAST COTTAGE DOME
WEST COTTAGE DOME
DAFF DOME
POTHOLE DOME
MARMOT DOME
FAIRVIEW DOME
THE LAMB
DRUG DOME
MARIUOLUMNE DOME
CATHEDRAL PEAK
LAKE OF THE DOMES
MEDLICOTT DOME
WEST FARTHING WALL
STICKS & STONES
DOZIER DOME
PYWIACK DOME
PENNYROYAL ARCHES
TENAYA PEAK

DODA DOME
DARKSIDE DOME
LAVA DOME
HAMMER DOME
NORTH WHIZZ DOME
SOUTH WHIZZ DOME
LOW PROFILE DOME
PHOBUS/DEIMOS CLIFF
POLLY DOME
MOUNTAINEER'S DOME
THE SHARK
HARLEQUIN DOME
STATELY PLEASURE DOME

TENAYA LAKE
TENAYA LAKE CAMPGROUND

TO YOSEMITE VALLEY

TUOLUMNE

SCALE IN MILES

N

0   ½

Pumper 5.10d (TR) This short, overhanging top rope crack is seen from the bridge over the South Fork of the Tuolumne River, 5¾ miles east along Hwy. 120 from Crane Flat Ranger Station.

1	Pleasant View Arete	3	Buckets of Blood
2	Battlescar Galactipus	4	Cattlestar Faticus

COYOTE ROCKS

These obscure, orange formations are found on the north side of Hwy. 120, approximately two miles west of the May Lake turnoff. Park in a paved turnout on the south side of the road, marked T-24. They are best approached from the west side.

Acme Crack 5.8 (PG, ?) This is the obvious straight-in, left-curving hand crack located left of the main Arête. Two pitches.

A **Pleasant View Arête** 5.9 (?, ?) Climb the Arête in two pitches over splendid rock to the summit of the lower formation.

B **Battlescar Galactipus** 5.9 (PG, ?) Above and right of **Pleasant View Arête** is an amphitheatre. Climb the most obvious crack.

Upper Wall from Notch 5.7 (?, ?) Attain the notch between the two formations and climb to the summit.

C **Buckets of Blood** 5.8 (?, ?) To the right of the amphitheater is a buttress. Follow this for two and a half pitches.

D **Cattlestar Faticus** 5.10b (?, ?) Start in the middle of the southeast face of the upper rock and climb 5.10a face to a ledge. A 5.9 pitch leads to a large ledge and alcove. The next pitch goes out a 5.10b roof, leading to easier climbing and the top.

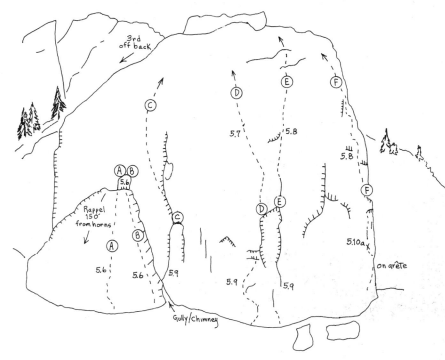

ROADRUNNER ROCK

This obscure rock is located on the lower south flank of Mt. Hoffman, just east of **Coyote Rocks.** Park at the May Lake Trail head which is about 12 miles west of the Tuolumne Meadows Store on Highway 120 and trend in a northwest direction for about one-half hour.

A **Cuckoo** 5.6 (PG, ?)
B **Beep-Beep** 5.6 (PG, ?)
C **Desert Highway** 5.9 (PG, ?)
D **Roadkill** 5.9 (R, ★ ★)
E **Roadrunner** 5.9 (PG ★ , ?)
F **Smiling at Wilee** 5.10a (PG, ★ ★)

OLMSTEAD AREA

A Osprey Overhang
1 Solstice
2 De Gaulle's Nose, Right Side
3 Overhang Over
4 Body Language
5 Greese Monkey
6 Age of Darkness

7 Air Cooled Unit
8 Short Change
9 Lord Caffeine
10 Ivory Tower – Center
11 Talk Dirty to Me
12 The Stanley Edge
13 Tideline

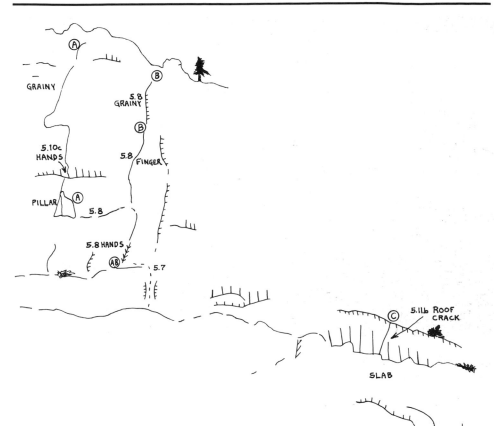

DE GAULLE'S NOSE

Park in a pave turnout ¼ mile west of Olmsted Point on the north side of the road. These climbs are on the cliff that is up left and high.

A   **Overhang Over** 5.10c (PG)
B   **Back to the Bar** 5.8 (? ?)
C   **Body Language** 5.11b (?, ★)

Point of No Return 5.10b (?, ?) Two short pitches, 150 feet up and right from **Body Language**. Pitch two is a hand crack that traverses right under a roof.

OSPREY OVERHANG

This is the prominent 150 foot cliff, capped by an overhang, that is visible on the skyline, east (right) of the De Gaulle's Nose area. Park ¼ mile west of Olmsted Point, in the turnout on the north side of the road, and follow a vague trail up the canyon for about ½ mile; then cut left through the brushy area.

A **Regular Route** 5.7 (PG, ★)
B **Ornithology** 5.11d (PG, ★ ★)
C **The Cage** 5.11b (PG, ★)

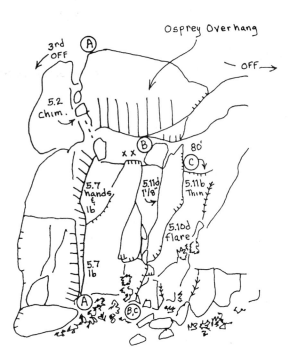

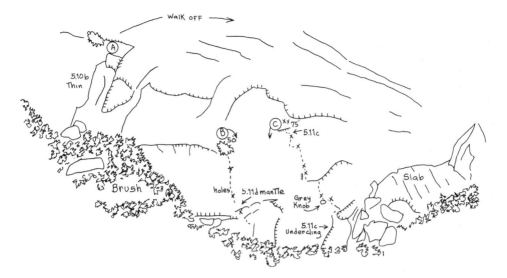

OLMSTEAD CANYON

APPROACH: These climbs are up and behind **Creature from the Black Lagoon**, where the slabs come down and right from **Body Language**.

A **Black Like Me** 5.10b (?)
B **Just What The Doctor Ordered** 5.11d (?)
C **Solstice** 5.11c (R) Pro: a few small to 2 inches.

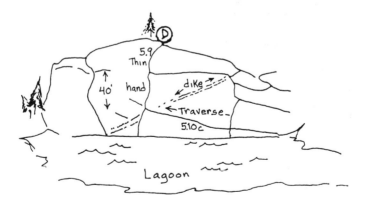

OLMSTEAD CANYON

D **Creature from the Black Lagoon** 5.10c (PG,) pro: ½ inch to 3 inch.

APPROACH: Park in a paved turnout ¼ mile west of Olmstead Point on the north side of the road. Olmstead Point is 10 miles west of the Tuolumne Meadows Store. Upon immediately entering Olmstead Canyon one will see a small pond down and left. C.F.B.L. is the small cliff rising out of the water.

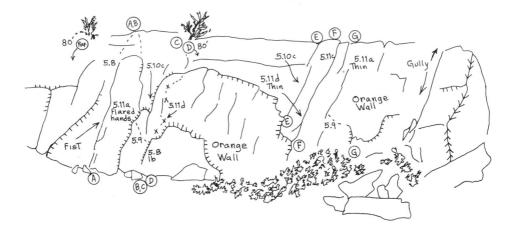

OLMSTEAD CANYON

Approximately ¼ mile west of the Olmsted Point turnout is a paved turnout on the north side of the road. Directly north is the **De Gaulle's Nose** climbing area. The following climbs are far down and right of De Gaulle's Nose. Follow the vague trail that leads up the canyon (northeast) for about ⅓ mile, then gain the large slabby area on the left side of the canyon.

A   **Grease Monkey** 5.8 (PG)
B   **Age of Darkness** 5.11a (PG)
C   **Lock of Ages** 5.10c (PG)
D   **Double Feature** 5.11d (PG, ★)
E   **Pressure Vessel** 5.10c (PG)
F   **Hot Box** 5.11d (PG, ★)
G   **Air-Cooled Unit** 5.11a (PG, ★)
H   **Easy Money** 5.11c (PG, ★)
I   **Duoich Mark** 5.9 (?)
J   **Reanimator** 5.12a (R)
K   **Short Change** 5.10a (PG, ★)
L   **Lord Caffeine** 5.10d (PG, ★ ★) Pro: ¼ inch to 3 inch, esp. 1 inch to 1½ inch.

M   **Ivory Tower Left** 5.8 (PG, ★)
N   **Ivory Tower Center** 5.10a (PG, ★)
O   **Ivory Tower Body-Double** 5.12a (PG)
P   **Miss Apprehension** 5.10a (PG)
Q   **Missile Toe** 5.10a (PG)
R   **Talk Dirty To Me** 5.9+ (PG)
S   **Enemy Within** 5.10b (PG, ★)
T   **The Thrill Is Gone** 5.10d (PG, ★)
U   **The Stanley Edge** 5.10c (PG)
V   **The Chamber** 5.7 (R, ★)
W   **Tideline** 5.11a (PG, ★ ★)
X   **Live Wire** 5.11b (R)

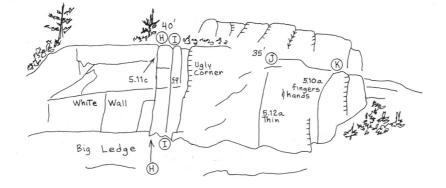

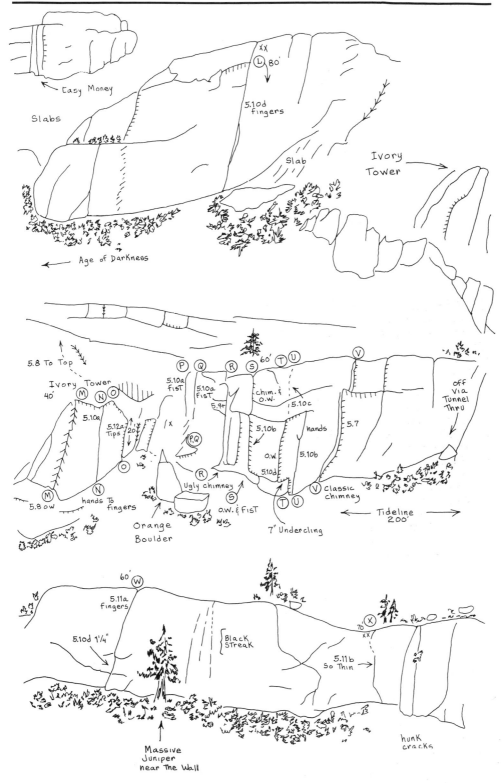

Easy Money

Slabs

xx
(L) 80'

5.10d
fingers

Slab

Ivory
Tower

Age of Darkness

5.8 To Top

Ivory Tower
40'

(M) (N) (O)

5.10a

5.12a
Tips

20'

x

(M)   (N)   (O)
5.8 ow   hands To
fingers

Orange
Boulder

(P) (Q)   (R) (S) 60' (T) (U)

5.10a
Fist

5.10a
Fist

5.9+

chim. &
o.w.

5.10c

(P,Q)

(R)

Ugly chimney

(S)
O.W. & Fist

5.10b   hands

O.W.   5.10b

5.10d

5.7

(V)

off
via
Tunnel
Thru

(V) Classic
chimney

(T) (U)

7" Undercling

Tideline
200'

60' (W)

5.11a
fingers

5.10d 1¼"

Black
Streak

70' (X)

xx

5.11b
So Thin

Massive
Juniper
near The Wall

hunk
cracks

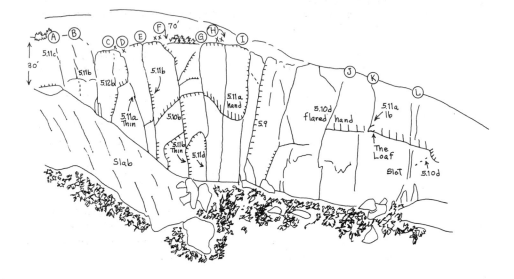

MURPHY CREEK

At the western end of Stately Pleasure Dome and on the Tenaya Lake side of Hwy. 120 is a parking and picnic area. The Murphy Creek trailhead is directly across the road. Follow the Murphy Creek Trail for approximately 1⅓ miles until you see this 80 foot cliff, about ¼ mile west of the trail. A great place for out-of-the-way top roping. Several short climbs are located on the four tiers of cliffs up and left from the Murphy Creek Wall.

A   **Sometimes a Great Notion** 5.11c (TR)
B   **Lizard Lips** 5.11b (TR)
C   **Precious Bodily Fluids** 5.12a (TR)
D   **Fluoridation** 5.11a (PG, ★)
E   **Auto Bond** 5.11b (PG, ★)
F   **Mandric** 5.10b (PG, ★)
G   **Gettin' in the Groove** 5.11d (PG, ★)
H   **Penguin Cafe** 5.11a (PG, ★)
I   **Gortlough RA** 5.9 (?)
J   **Party Time** 5.10d (?)
K   **Pinch A Loaf** 5.11a (?)
L   **Derbyshire** 5.10d (?) Pro: incl. 2# 4's

STATELY PLEASURE DOME

A very popular dome with excellent views of Tenaya Lake, park on the north side of the road about 7.5 miles west of the Tuolumne Meadows Store where the dome abuts the lake.

DESCENT   The descent from the routes of Stately Pleasure is as follows. Contour improbable slabs left towards a distinctive headwall that gets progressively larger to the west. Skirt the base of this wall via friction until easier slabs lead to the road.

Black Angel 5.11a (PG, ★ ★ ?) Where the west end of the dome meets Tenaya Lake is a short steep wall with a black streak. Several hundred feet above the road a right slanting lieback/finger crack intersects the streak. Pro: small to 2½ inch, especially ½ inch to 1 inch.

Dead Next Door 5.9 (PG) A short, one pitch hand crack is located approximately 30 feet left of **Death Crack**.

Death Crack 5.11d (PG, ★ ★ ★) This intimidating crack is located 300 yards right of **Black Angel**. It can be seen as it looms above the descent route for many of the subsequent climbs. Pro: 2½ inch to 6 inch.

The Ledge 5.11a (PG/R, ★) This climb is located 150 feet right of **Death Crack**, just right of a large right leaning diehidral. Follow three bolts up a ledge that diagonals left.

Turkey Trot 5.6 This route begins on the sandy ledges about 50 feet left of the **Kamps-Couch** route. Go straight up the obvious ramp between two crack systems. Bolt protected, but take nuts.

The following climbs are located on the headwall several hundred feet above the **Great White Book**.

Your Soft Sundae 5.10a (X, ?) solo 40 feet just left of a prominent white dike.

My Dove Bear 5.9 (X, ?) solo Follows the prominent white dike.

Feral Waife 5.12a Climb up the prominent black streak, 25 feet right of **My Dove Bear**, to a large boulder above two horizontal cracks (t.r.).

STATELY PLEASURE DOME – West Side

1 Starts for various easy 5th class climbs
2 Kamps-Couch
3 White Flake
4 West Country
5 Hermaphrodite Flake
6 Eunuch
7 Table of Contents
8 Great White Book
9 Get Slick
10 South Crack
11 The Ledge

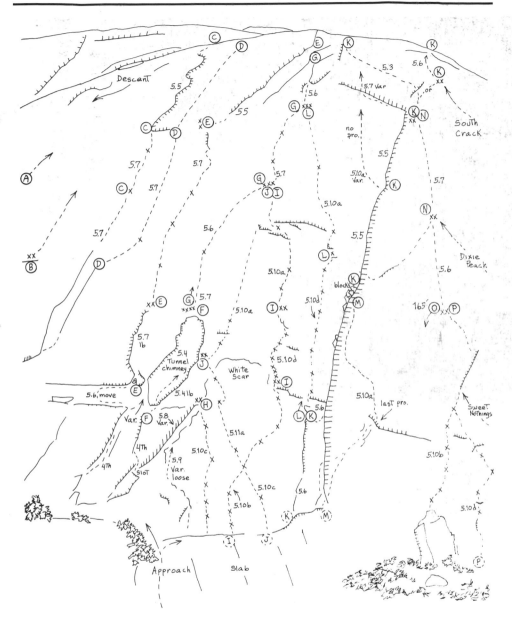

STATELY PLEASURE DOME — WEST

A **Far West** 5.6 (R)
B **Kamps-Couch** 5.7 (?, ?)
C **White Flake** 5.7 (R, ★)
D **The Shadow Nose** 5.7 (?, ?)
E **West Country** 5.7 (PG, ★ ★)
F **Hermaphrodite Flake** 5.4 (PG, ★)
G **Eunuch** 5.7 (R, ★ ★)
H **Footnote** 5.10c (PG/R, ★)

I **Table of Contents** 5.10d (R, ★ ★)
J **Cross Reference** 5.11a (R, ★)
K **Great White Book** 5.6 (R, ★ ★ ★)
L **Preface** 5.10d (R)
M **Great White Book Arête** 5.10a (X)
N **Mosquito** 5.7 (R)
O **Get Slick** 5.10b (R, ★)
P **G & S Route** 5.10d (R, ?)

STATELY PLEASURE DOME — EAST

A **Sweet Nothings** 5.10c (R, ★)
B **Climbing Club** 5.10a (R, ★)
C **Malletosis** 5.10+ (R)
D **Dixie Peach** 5.9 (PG, ★)
E **South Crack** 5.8 emphasize pro ¼ inch to 1 inch (R, ★ ★ ★)
F **Quiet Desperation** 5.9 (R, ★)
G **Barely Anything** 5.10c (PG/R, ★)
H **Prince of Pleasure** 5.10d (missing 2 hangers) (PG, ★)
I **Step It Up and Go** 5.10c (PG/R, ★)

J **Foolish Pleasures** 5.11a (PG/R, ★)
K **Miss Adventure** 5.10d (R, ★ ★)
L **Way We Could Have Been** 5.10c (?, ★)
M **The Way We Were** 5.10a (PG/R,)
N **Daddy's Little Girl** 5.10d (R, ★ ★)
O **Dreams** 5.11c (PG, ★)
P **Helter Skelter** 5.13a (?, ?)
Q **Arch Rival** 5.11c Pro: tiny to 1½ inch (PG, ★ ★)

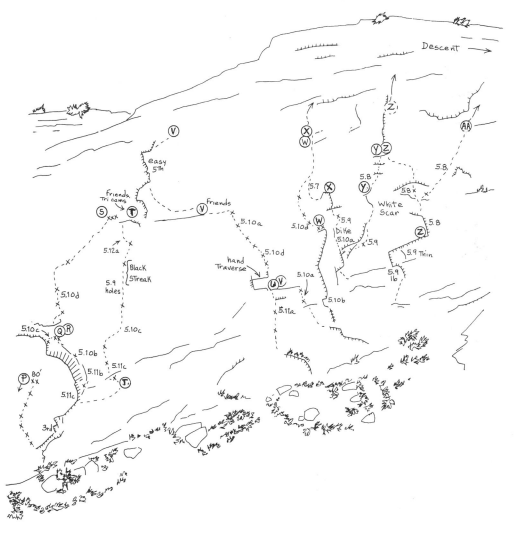

R **Immaculate Deception** 5.11b Pro: tiny to 1½ inch (PG, ★)

S **Cleared For Take Off** 5.10d (R)

T **Grace Under Pressure** 5.12a (R/X, ★★)

U **Goldline** 5.11a (?, ?)

V **Turning Japanese** 5.10d Pro: tiny to 2½ inch (PG, ★)

W **Hooker** 5.10d (R, ★)

X **Shy Tuna** 5.10a (PG/R)

Y **Babe Roof** 5.9 (PG/R)

Z **Camel Walk** 5.9 (PG/R)

AA **Botch** 5.9 (R)

The Prime Chopper 5.11 (R, ?) This route is 200 feet right of **Botch** and ascends a thin face with 4 bolts.

Flat Top 5.10 (?, ?) About 30 feet right of the **Prime Chopper**, follow some flakes up to a dike with 2 bolts.

STATELY PLEASURE DOME — East Side

1 Death Crack
2 Hermaphrodite Flake
3 Great White Book
4 Get Slick
5 South Crack
6 Quiet Desperation
7 Barely Anything
8 Step It Up and Go
9 The Way We Were
10 Dreams
11 Arch Rival
12 Turning Japanese
13 Camel Walk

HARLEQUIN DOME
1 Trilogy
2 Hoodwink
3 The Sting
4 No Rock Nazis
5 By Hook or by Crook
6 Sausalito Archie's Overhang
7 Third World

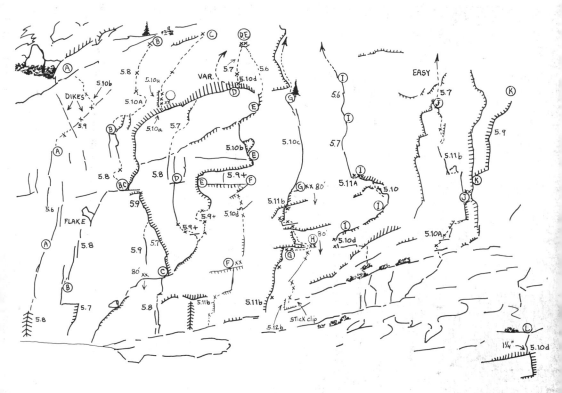

HARLEQUIN DOME

This dome offers a variety of climbs, including several steep routes that snake their way through roofs.

APPROACH: From the parking lot at the east end of Tenaya Lake, hike up the slabs on the north side of the road and gain a inobvious notch through the headwall directly below **By Hook Or By Crook**.

Descend via the broad gully between Stately Pleasure and Harlequin Domes.

Harlequin Route 5.7 (PG/R, ★)   This route avoids the more obvious difficulties of the cliff. Climb various cracks on the left margin of the dome to attain the second belay of **Hoodwink**. Traverse right across conspicuous ledges beneath the large roof to join the last pitch of **The Sting**.

A **Trilogy** 5.10b (R)
B **Harlot** 5.10a   pro: ½ inch to 2½ inch (R)
C **Hoodwink** 5.10a (PG, ★ ★)
D **Rock Lobster** 5.10d   pro: to 3 inch; missing hangers last pitch (PG, ★)
E **The Sting** 5.10b   pro: tiny to 2 inch (PG, ★ ★)
F **No Rock Nazis** 5.11b (PG)
G **By Hook or by Crook** 5.11b pro: tiny to 2½ inch (PG, ★ ★ ★)
H **Heat Sensitive** 5.12b (PG, ★) Stick clip 1st bolt.
I **Sausalito Archie's Overhang** 5.11a (R)
J **Third World** 5.11b   pro: tiny to 2½ inch (PG, ★)
K **The Whore That Ate Chicago** 5.9 (?)
L **Chinese Handcuffs** 5.10d pro: tiny to 3 inch (PG, ★)

THE SHARK
1 Vicious Thing
2 Curve Like Her
3 Corn Hole
4 Bushes and Buckets
5 Archille's Last Stand
6 Fairies Wear Boots

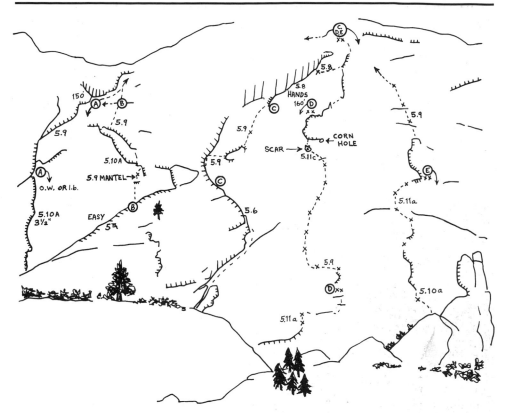

THE SHARK

A **Vicious Thing**   5.10c   pro: to 3½ especially 2 inch to 3½ inch
B **Flipper**   5.10a   (R)
C **Curve Like Her**   5.9 (R, ★)
D **Corn Hole**   5.11c   (R, ★)
E **Bushes and Buckets**   5.11a   (R)

Tenaya Lake Bouldering   This area encompasses the boulders from the parking lot at the east end of Tenaya Lake to the western margin of Mountaineer's Dome.

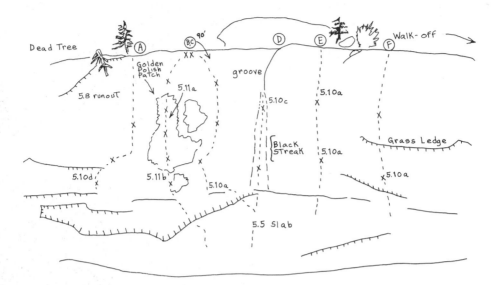

GUPPIE WALL

This 90-foot high gold polished cliff is located directly below The Shark and is best approached from the eastern end of the parking lot tht is at the east end of Tenaya Lake. Fun little area for some top roping or short end of the day leads.

A **Gimme Some Slack** 5.10d (R)
B **Panning for Nuggets** 5.11b (R,★)
C **Pokin' the Pup** 5.10a (R)
D **Achilles Last Stand** 5.10a (R, ★)
E **Fairies Wear Boots** 5.10a (R, ★)
F **Astrovan** 5.10a (R)

MOUNTAINEER'S DOME

A CIRCLE A WALL
1 Undisputed Truth
2 Thin Air
3 Tourist Trap
4 Faux Pas
5 Pippin
6 Paiste Formula
7 Paris is Burning
8 Go for the Gold
9 Realm of the Absurd
10 Happy Hour
11 Vice Gripped
12 American Wet Dream
13 Bastard from the Bush
14 Mere Image

MOUNTAINEER'S DOME

Found on the north side of the road about 7 miles west of the Tuolumne Meadow Store. The **Circle a Wall** is down low and just east of Mountaineer's Dome. The low angle area east of here and west of the block is **The Bunny Slopes.**

A **Undisputed Truth** 5.10a (PG/R)
B **Thin Air** 5.9 (R)
C **Namche Bazzar** 5.9 (R)
D **Golden Years** 5.12a Top rope
E **Tourist Trap** 5.10d (R)
F **Faux Pas** 5.9 (PG, ★)
G **Pippin** 5.9   pro: small to 3 inch (PG/R, ★)
H **Paiste Formula** 5.11c (PG, ★★)
I **Groundout** 5.11d (R/X, ★)
J **Double Eagle** 5.11b (R, ★)
K **Paris Is Burning** 5.11b (?, ★)
L **Go for the Gold** 5.11b (R, ★)
M **Realm of the Absurd** 5.11d (R, ★)
N **Happy Hour** 5.10b (PG/R, ★)
O **Dirty Dream** 5.11b (?, ?)
P **Vice Gripped** 5.10c (R, ★)
Q **How Does It Feel?** 5.11a (R, ★)
R **American Wet Dream** 5.10b   pro: tiny to 3 inch (PG, ★★)
S **American Wet Dike** 5.10b (?, ?)
T **Bastard from the Bush** 5.11a (R/X)
U **Crag Witch** 5.10 (?)

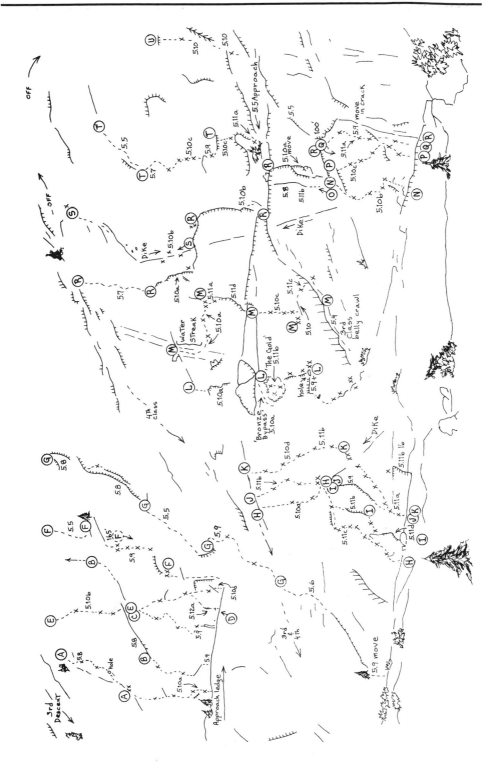

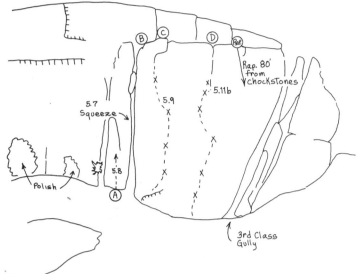

CIRCLE A WALL

APPROACH: This is the steepest small cliff on the far right side of Mountaineer's Dome where it meets low angle slabs and is just above a road cut.

A   **Levy's Lament** 5.8 (PG)
B   **Rodeo Revolution** 5.7 (PG)
C   **Joe Mamba** 5.9 (PG/R, ★)
D   **Apex Predator** 5.11b (PG/R, ★)

Delta Squeeze 5.8 Several hundred feet up and right from The **American Wet Dream** is a section containing many broken roofs. In the vicinity of an orange block is a recess. **Delta Squeeze** is the short chimney on the right side of the recess.

Lieback Detector 5.9 A short distance to the right of **Delta Squeeze** is a right facing, arching, grass-filled crack.

Sunny Delight 5.8 This route is located on a small apron 300 feet left of **Pippin** and below and left of the ledge the starts **Thin Air** and **Faux Pas**. Start in the middle of the apron and climb past a bolt to a ledge. Continue past three more bolts through a prominent polished area that leads to easier climbing and the top.

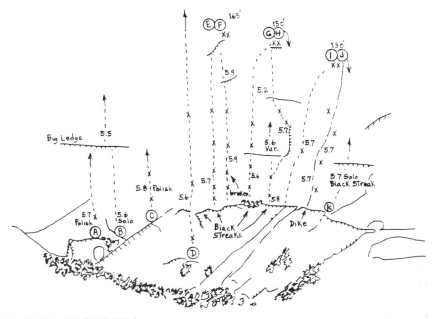

THE BUNNY SLOPES

APPROACH: These are the low angle slabs between Mountaineer's Dome and **The Block**.

A **Cool Meditation** 5.7 (R)
B **Walkman** 5.6 solo (X)
C **Hit Or Miss** 5.8 (R)
D **Black Uhuru** 5.6 (R/X)
E **Wild in the Streaks** 5.7 (PG, ★)
F **Black Diamond** 5.9 (X)
G **Hot Crossed Buns** 5.6 (PG, ★)
H **Biscuit and Gravy** 5.8 (PG, ★)
I **Raindance** 5.7 (R/X)
J **Mere Image** 5.7 (PG/R, ★)
K **Solo** 5.7 (X)

THE BLOCK AREA

Found here are several crack and face climbs, including the incredible 20-foot **High Heels** roof. Located on the north side of the road directly across from the western end of Pywiack Dome, park at the west end of Pywiack Dome about 6.5 miles west of the Tuolumne Meadows Store.

1	Hammered	4	High Heels
2	The Block, Direct	5	Public Enemy
3	Push-Push	6	Fuel Rod

The Knobs Bouldering   This prolific area is located on the north side of Hwy. 120, 1/2 mile east of Pywiack. The boulders strewn about this granite "pavement" feature steep climbing on protruding feldspar cystals, characteristic of many of the climbs of the area.

Workout Man 5.11 (TR) In a blocky area straight uphill from **The Knobs**, hand traverse out the left edge of a triangular roof. Continue up and right, face climbing on knobs.

THE BLOCK AREA

A **Don't Exchange Bodily Fluids** 5.10a (R)
B **Drafted** 5.9 (R,)
C **Public Enemy** 5.11d (PG, ★)
D **Hammered** 5.10c (R/X)
E **The Block, Left** 5.9 Pro to 6 inches (PG)
   The Block, Center 5.11a Pro: 1 KB; many tiny wired nuts (R/X).

The Block, Right 5.8 (R)
F **Can't Say** 5.10c (R)
G **Grass Roots** 5.10c (?, ?)
H **Push-Push** 5.11a (PG, ★ ★)
I **Fuel Rod** 5.10b (PG, ★)
J **High Heels** 5.12b Pro: tiny to 2 ½inches (PG, ★ ★ ★)

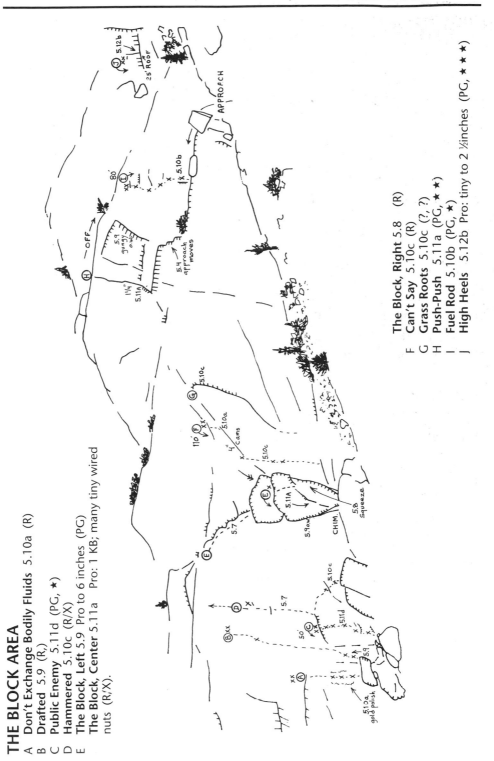

PHOBOS/DEIMOS

This is one of the few true cliffs of the Tuolumne region. This long band of orange and white rock is directly across from Pywiack and high above the road about 6.2 miles west from the Tuolumne Meadows Store. Park directly across from the eastern end of Pywiack. A spring emanating from a small stone wall is a useful landmark. Avoid heavy brush from this point by hiking diagonally to the west before proceeding upward. Climbing is characterized by steep, classic cracks.

1	**Universal Corner**	6	**Hobbitation**
2	**Phobos**	7	**Deimos**
3	**Blues Riff**	8	**Love Supreme**
4	**Gold Finger**	9	**Laser Blade**
5	**The Cooler**	10	**Ugly Arete**

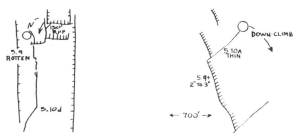

Transformer   5.10d (PG, ★)   This is ¼ mile est of Phobos/Deimos. Pro: several small to 3½ inch.

Five-Volt Zener   5.10+ (PG, ★)   This sits on the steep wall 700 feet right of **Transformer**. Pro: esp. 3½ inch.

Galen's Crack   5.10c (TR)   This is a 30 foot hand to off-width crack located on the north side of Hwy. 120, directly across from the **The Yawn**, on Medlicott Dome.

Falkenstein Face   5.10+ (TR)   This is the overhanging face to the right of **Galen's Crack**.

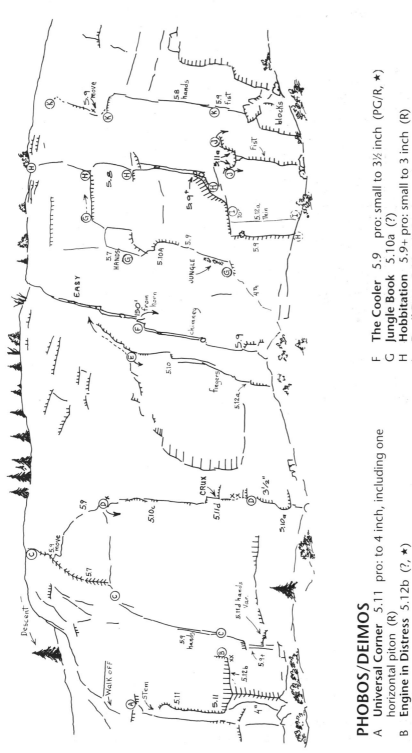

PHOBOS/DEIMOS

A **Universal Corner** 5.11 pro: to 4 inch, including one horizontal piton (R)

B **Engine in Distress** 5.12b (?, ★)

C **Phobos** 5.9 pro: to 3 inch (PG, ★ ★ ★)

D **Blues Riff** 5.11c pro: to 3 inch especially ¾ inch to 2 inch (PG, ★ ★ ★)

E **Gold Finger** 5.12a pro: several 1/2 inch-1 inch (PG, ★ ★ ★)

F **The Cooler** 5.9 pro: small to 3½ inch (PG/R, ★)

G **Jungle Book** 5.10a (?)

H **Hobbitation** 5.9+ pro: small to 3 inch (R)

I **Devil Dog** 5.12a (PG, ★)

J **Compared to What** 5.11a pro: tiny to 3½ inch (PG,)

K **Deimos** 5.9 (PG, ★ ★ ★)

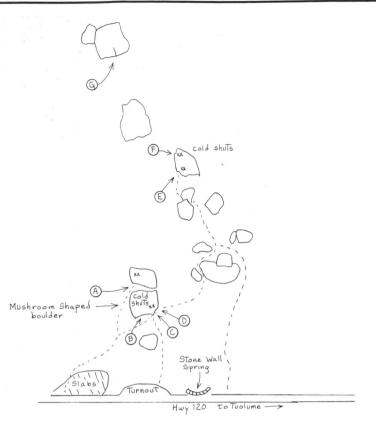

THE ARENA

Four short killer sport climbs and one of the hardest cracks of Tuolumne bedeck the arena. Park at a paved turnout with a spring on the north side of the road about 6.2 miles west from the Tuolumne Meadows Store and just east of Pywiack Dome. A short hike up past the spring brings you to the **Ugly Arête.**

A   **Double Take** 5.10d (PG)
B   **Roadkill** 5.11c (PG, ★)
C   **Ugly Arête** 5.12a (PG, ★)
D   **Carcass** 5.12b 3 bolts (PG)
E   **Lazer Blade** 5.12d (PG, ★ ★)
F   **Quick Release** 5.12b (PG, ★ ★)
G   **Love Supreme** 5.13 (PG, ★ ★)

LOW PROFILE DOME

Located on the north side of Hwy. 120, ¾ mile east of Pywiack Dome and about 5.5 miles west of the Tuolumne Meadows store, this is the low, dark formation, with several conspicuous horizontal slashes.

1	Hurricane Betsy	6	Golfer's Route
2	Ages Apart	7	Darth Vader's Revenge
3	Black Widow	8	Shit Hooks
4	Get Sick	9	Memo from Loyd
5	Steep Thrills		

These climbs are located several hundred yards uphill from the left end of **Low Profile Dome**.

Gold Standard 5.10c (?, ?) This is a 2-bolt climb left of a low angle slab.

Pepe Le Peu 5.10d (?, ?) Located 200 feet right of **Gold Standard**, follow two bolts up a slab to a roof, then over the roof past a bush.

Tom Tom 5.10a (?, ?) Climb up a hand crack then past two bolts, 200 feet right of **Pepe Le Peu.**

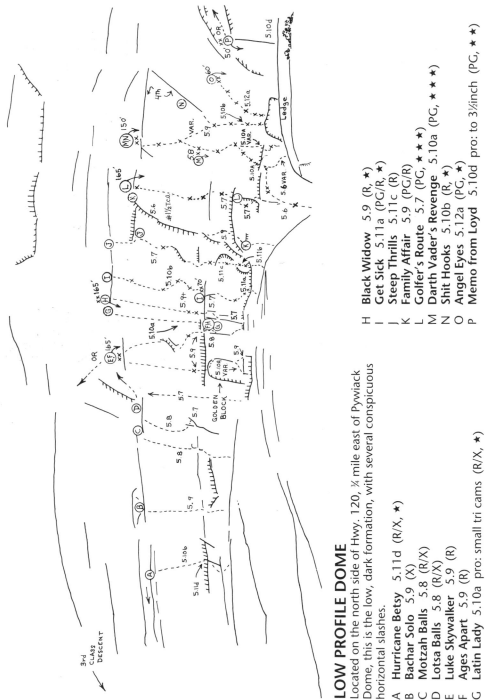

LOW PROFILE DOME

Located on the north side of Hwy. 120, ¾ mile east of Pywiack Dome, this is the low, dark formation, with several conspicuous horizontal slashes.

A **Hurricane Betsy** 5.11d (R/X, ★)
B **Bachar Solo** 5.9 (X)
C **Motzah Balls** 5.8 (R/X)
D **Lotsa Balls** 5.8 (R/X)
E **Luke Skywalker** 5.9 (R)
F **Ages Apart** 5.9 (R)
G **Latin Lady** 5.10a pro: small tri cams (R/X, ★)

H **Black Widow** 5.9 (R, ★)
I **Get Sick** 5.11a (PG/R, ★)
J **Steep Thrills** 5.11c (R)
K **Family Affair** 5.9 (PG/R)
L **Golfer's Route** 5.7 (PG, ★ ★ ★)
M **Darth Vader's Revenge** 5.10a (PG, ★ ★ ★)
N **Shit Hooks** 5.10b (R, ★)
O **Angel Eyes** 5.12a (PG, ★)
P **Memo from Loyd** 5.10d pro: to 3½inch (PG, ★ ★)

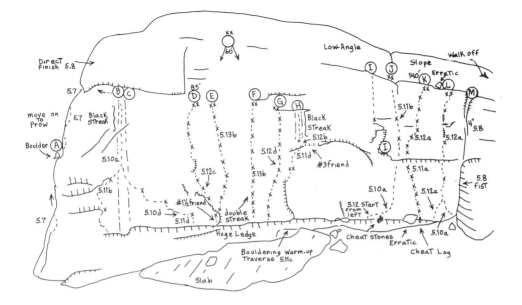

SOUTH WHIZZ DOME

The Whizz Domes are 150-foot cliffs that face to the northwest. They can be hard to find due to the dense forest. Park in a paved turnout on the north side of the road about 5 miles west from the Tuolumne Store and across from the eastern end of Medlicott Dome. From this turnout hike northwest past a small meadow and then through thick forest over several small granite escarpments for about half a mile. Don't go to far left.

A **Prow** 5.7 (R, ★)
B **Decoy** 5.11b (X)
C **Start Bouldering** 5.11d (X, ★)
D **Shadow Warriors** 5.12c (PG, ★ ★ ★)
E **Super Sonic** 5.13b (PG, ★ ★)
F **Love Sexy** 5.13b (PG, ★ ★)
G **Fame and Fortune** 5.12d (PG, ★ ★)
H **Body and Soul** 5.12 (X, ★ ★ ★)
I **Cheat Stone** 5.12 (X, ★ ★ ★)
J **Blackout** 5.11b (X, ★ ★ ★)
K **Body Count** 5.12a (PG, ★ ★)
L **Countdown** 5.12a (X, ★)
M **Rivendell Crack** 5.8 pro: 3 inch (PG)

NORTH WHIZZ DOMES

A **Cuckoo's Nest** 5.9 (R)
B **Ease On It** 5.10c (R)
C **Knob Roulette** 5.10d (R/X)
North Face Route 5.7 (R/X, ?)
Start climbing behind a detached flake near the right side of the north face. Three pitches of mostly face climbing wander up past several horizontal cracks which provide marginal protection. Pro: tiny to 2½ inch

West Side Route 5.6 (?, ?) On the left side of the west face is an unmistakable cleft which breaks the summit area. Ascend a chimney to a long sloping ramp. Follow this ramp right to reach the final chimney that leads to the summit.

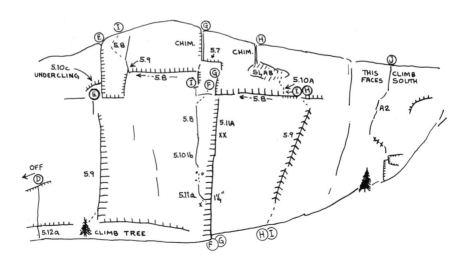

D **The Deviate** 5.12a (PG)
E **Thy Will Be Done** 5.10c (PG, ★)
F **Twister** 5.11a (?, ?)
G **Handbook** 5.11a pro: tiny to 3½ inch (PG, ★ ★ ★)
H **Deception** 5.10a (PG/R, ★)
I **Take a Whizz** 5.9 (PG)
J **Gee Whizz** A2 (PG, ★)

HAMMER DOME (also MICRO DOME AND RIVER WALL)

This is the small, low cliff located on the northeastern side of Cathedral Creek about 1 mile downstream from Highway 120. About 3.6 miles west from the Tuolumne Meadows Store and just past Daff Dome is a dirt turnout by a 4-foot road-cut cliff. Immediately below the road is Cathedral Creek. Follow this downstream first passing Micro Dome (4 minutes out), then the River Wall (15 minutes out) to Hammer Dome. 20 min. All of these, except Johnny Rock, are on the right side of the river.

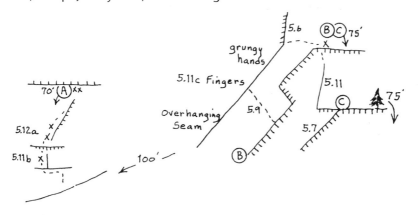

DOWNSTREAM FROM HAMMER DOME

These climbs face west, ½ mile downstream.

A **Beyond A Shadow of Doubt** 5.12a pro: small to 1½ inch. (R, ★)
B **Motor Home for Midgets** 5.11c (?, ?)
C **Low Budget** 5.11 (?, ?)
Johnny Rock 5.11c (R/X, ★) This one bolt, one pitch climb is on a dome 1/2 mile downstream from **Motor Home for Midgets**.

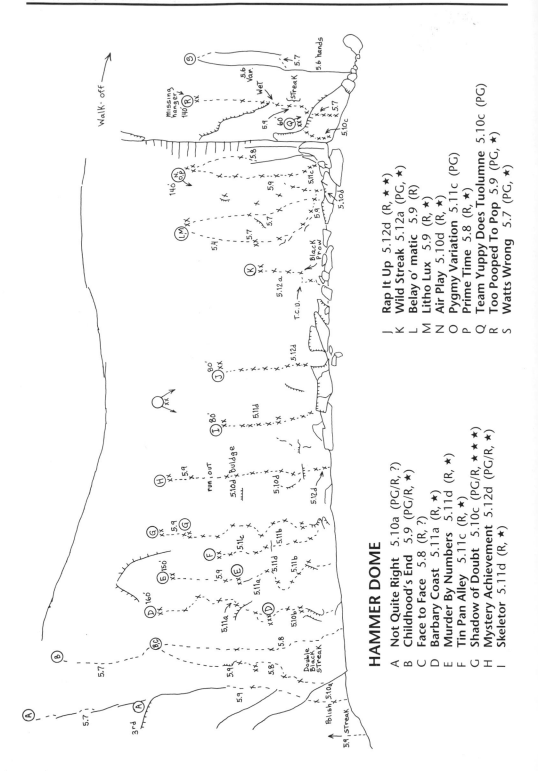

HAMMER DOME

A Not Quite Right 5.10a (PG/R, ?)
B Childhood's End 5.9 (PG/R, ★)
C Face to Face 5.8 (R, ?)
D Barbary Coast 5.11a (R, ★)
E Murder By Numbers 5.11d (R, ★)
F Tin Pan Alley 5.11c (R, ★)
G Shadow of Doubt 5.10c (PG/R, ★ ★ ★)
H Mystery Achievement 5.12d (PG/R, ★)
I Skeletor 5.11d (R, ★)
J Rap It Up 5.12d (R, ★ ★)
K Wild Streak 5.12a (PG, ★)
L Belay o' matic 5.9 (R)
M Litho Lux 5.9 (R, ★)
N Air Play 5.10d (R, ★)
O Pygmy Variation 5.11c (PG)
P Prime Time 5.8 (R, ★)
Q Team Yuppy Does Tuolumne 5.10c (PG)
R Too Pooped To Pop 5.9 (PG, ★)
S Watts Wrong 5.7 (PG, ★)

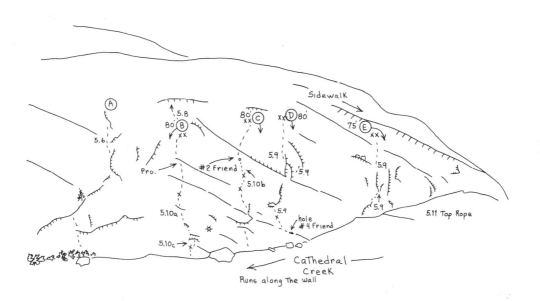

RIVER WALL

A **The S.S. Minow** 5.6 (PG)
B **Whipped Cream** 5.10c (PG, ★)
C **Pajama People** 5.10b (PG, ★)
D **Boat Party** 5.9 (PG)
E **Zulu Lulu** 5.9 (PG)

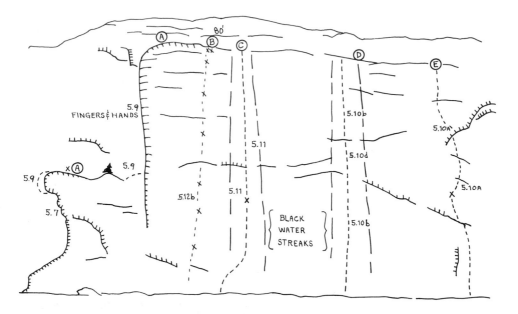

LAVA DOME

Follow the approach for Hammer Dome. Reach the indistinct small domes that are northeast of Hammer Dome by moving up intricate slopes from a point ¼ mile east. These routes lie on the northwest side and therefore cannot be seen until arrival. (The dome is the 8753 foot mark, north of Hammer Dome, found on the USGS Tuolumne Meadows Quadrangle.

A **Stick and Span** 5.9   pro: small to 2 inch, especially small to 1¼ inch (PG, ★)
B **Shut It Up** 5.12b T.C.U.'s. (PG, ★)
C **The Flash** 5.11 (R/X, ★)
D **Movement in Camouflage** 5.10d   pro: friends useful (R, ★ ★)
E **Summertime** 5.10a (R/X, ?)

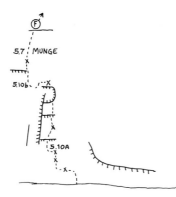

ALCATRAZ ROCK

This is the small dome east of Lava Dome.

F **The Great Escape** 5.10b

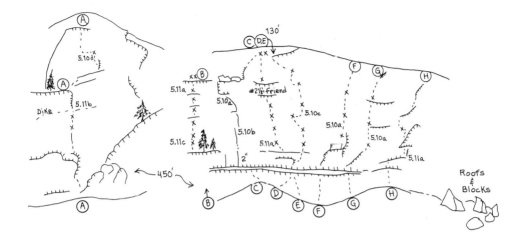

DOME PERIGNON

After passing Micro Dome going down Cathedral Creek one will come to some slabs on the right. Follow these uphill to the backside of this dome which faces northwest. Dome Perignon is somewhat west of Dark Side Dome.

A   **Night and Day** 5.11b (?, ?)
B   **Torque Yer Mudda** 5.11c (PG, ★)
C   **Space Sluts in the Scammer** 5.10b (PG)
D   **Mike and Urmy** 5.11a (PG, ★)
E   **Friggin For Higgins** 5.10c (PG, ★)
F   **Urban Perversion** 5.10a (R)
G   **Charriots of the Todds** 5.10a (R)
H   **Pie in the Sky** 5.11a (?, ?)

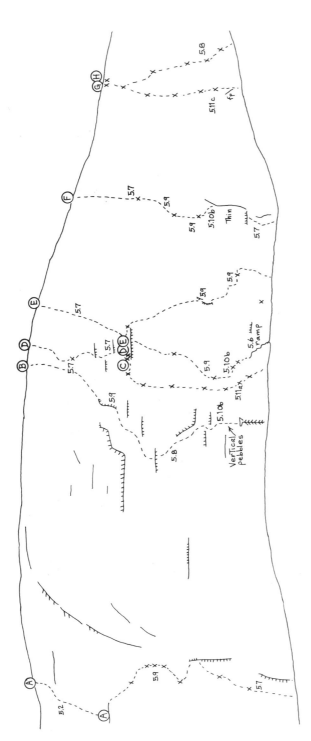

DARK SIDE DOME

Follow the Hammer Dome approach for about 3/4 mile. Gain the north side of Cathedral Creek and wander north up slabs, aiming for this small north facing dome. This is the most prominent small dome just east of the 8753 mark on the USGS Tuolumne Meadows Quadrangle.

A **Pebble Beach** 5.9 (PG/R)
B **Inner Vision** 5.10b (R/X, ?)
C **Walking The Dog** 5.11a (R, ?)
D **Voice of the Crags** 5.10b (PG/R, ★)
E **Brainwave** 5.9 (R/X, ?)
F **Shot in the Dark** 5.10b   pro: tiny nuts (PG/R, ★)
G **Batteries Not Included** 5.11c (?, ★)
H **Who's The Bosch** 5.8 (?, ★)

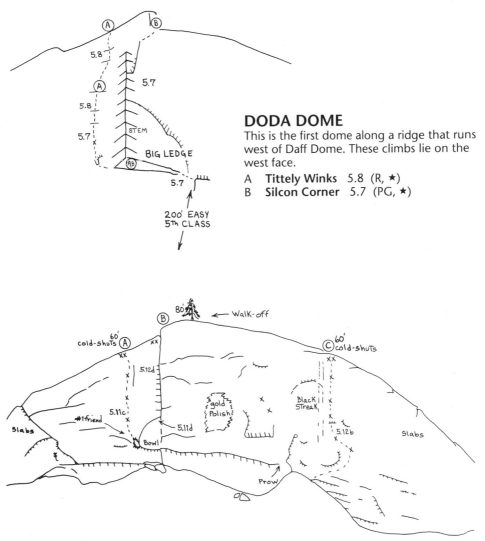

DODA DOME

This is the first dome along a ridge that runs west of Daff Dome. These climbs lie on the west face.

A **Tittely Winks** 5.8 (R, ★)
B **Silcon Corner** 5.7 (PG, ★)

MICRO DOME

This small dome is found on the northeast side of Cathedral Creek. Park in a turnout just west of Daff Dome on the right (north) side of the road. Immediately below is Cathedral Creek. Follow this downstream on its right side for 4 minutes.

A **Midnight Hour** 5.11c (PG)
B **Positivity** 5.12d pro: RP's, T.C.U., 3 friend (PG, ★ ★)
C **Rebel Yell** 5.12b (PG, ★ ★)

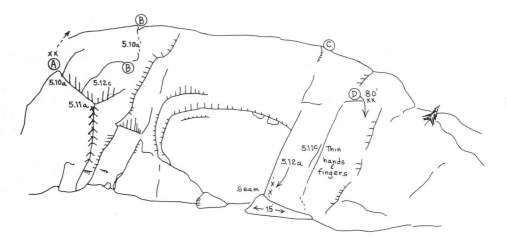

BEARDED CLAM CLIFF

These climbs are located on a cliff that sits several hundred feet below the west face of Daff Dome. **Bearded Clam, Cowabunga** and **Into the Void** are on the northwest end of the cliff; The **Western Front** is on the extreme southeast end, only a few minutes from the road.

A **Bearded Clam** 5.11a (PG, ★)
B **Cowabunga** 5.12c (PG, ★ ★)

C **Reptilian Brain Syndrome** 5.12a (R)
D **Into The Void** 5.11c (PG/R, ★ ★)

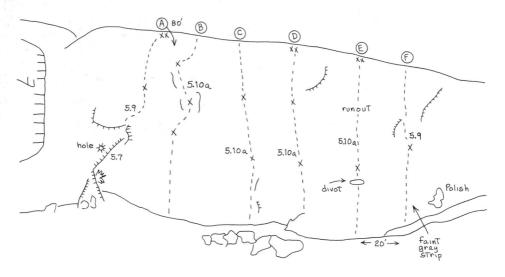

THE WESTERN FRONT

A **Green Eggs and Ham** 5.9 (PG/R)
B **March of Dimes** 5.10a (PG/R)
C **New Tricks for Old Dogs** 5.10a (R)

D **Touch of Grey** 5.10a (R)
E **Ace in the Hole** 5.10a (R/X)
F **Deadheads Delight** 5.9 (R)

DAFF DOME AND SURROUNDING AREA

A   MICRO DOME
B   WESTERN FRONT
C   COWABUNGA
D   WEST COTTAGE
E   MT. CONNESS
F   EAST COTTAGE DOME

1   West Crack
2   Crescent Arch
3   R.C.A.
4   El Condor
5   Fingertips
6   Great Circle

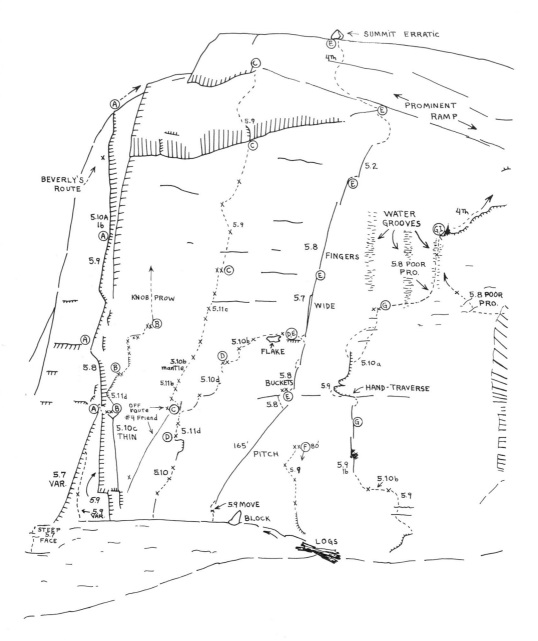

DAFF DOME — WEST FACE (LEFT)

A **Cooke Booke** 5.10a (PG, ★ ★)
B **Bombs Over Tokyo** 5.12c (?, ?)
C **Wienie Roast** 5.11c (R, ★)
D **Sunny Side Down** 5.11d (R)

E **West Crack** 5.9 (PG, ★ ★ ★)
F **Witch o' The West** 5.9 (PG/R)
G **Black Bart** 5.10b (R, ★)

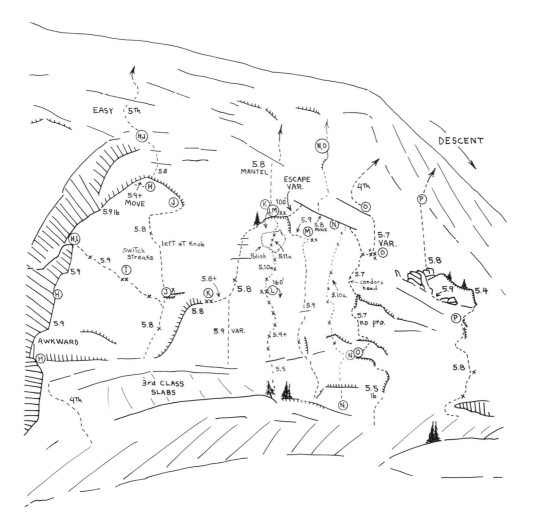

DAFF DOME — WEST FACE (RIGHT)

DESCENT   Hike off the south side of the dome down 3rd and 4th class slabs. After about 400 feet move west onto easier slabs.

H   **Crescent Arch** 5.9+ (PG, ★ ★ ★)
I   **Tales from the Crypt** 5.9 (R)
J   **Apparition** 5.8 (R, ★)
K   **R.C.A.** 5.8 (R, ★)

L   **Chvchicháschtli** 5.11a (PG/R, ★)
M   **Grey Ghost** 5.9 (R/X, ?)
N   **Fool's Gold** 5.10a (PG/R, ★)
O   **El Condor** 5.8 (R/X, ★ ★)
P   **T.H. Sea** 5.9 (PG/R)

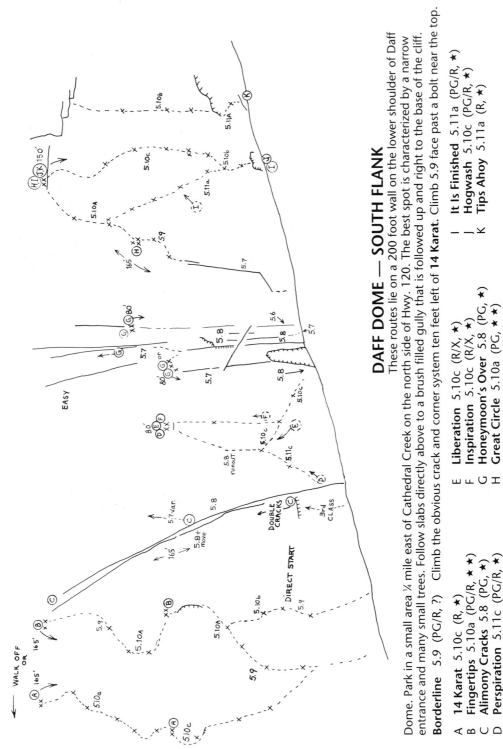

DAFF DOME — SOUTH FLANK

These routes lie on a 200 foot wall on the lower shoulder of Daff Dome. Park in a small area ¼ mile east of Cathedral Creek on the north side of Hwy. 120. The best spot is characterized by a narrow entrance and many small trees. Follow slabs directly above to a brush filled gully that is followed up and right to the base of the cliff.

Borderline 5.9 (PG/R, ?)   Climb the obvious crack and corner system ten feet left of **14 Karat**. Climb 5.9 face past a bolt near the top.

A   **14 Karat** 5.10c (R, ★)
B   **Fingertips** 5.10a (PG/R, ★ ★)
C   **Alimony Cracks** 5.8 (PG, ★)
D   **Perspiration** 5.11c (PG/R, ★)

E   **Liberation** 5.10c (R/X, ★)
F   **Inspiration** 5.10c (R/X, ★)
G   **Honeymoon's Over** 5.8 (PG, ★)
H   **Great Circle** 5.10a (PG, ★ ★)

I   **It Is Finished** 5.11a (PG/R, ★)
J   **Hogwash** 5.10c (PG/R, ★)
K   **Tips Ahoy** 5.11a (R, ★)

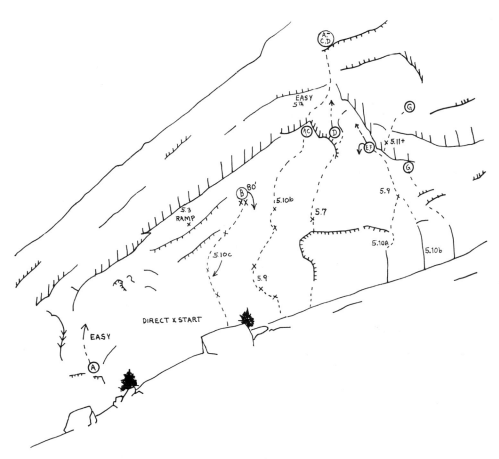

DAFF DOME — EAST FACE

To approach these climbs, continue up from the south flank approach or take a more direct line as follows: Park at the Fairview Dome parking area approximately ½ mile east of Cathedral Creek, on the south side of Hwy. 120. Hike directly up through the woods and across some slabs, aiming for the east face.

A **Glee** 5.3 (?, ?)
B **Fireworks** 5.10c (R)
C **Crow's Feet** 5.10b (R)
D **Face Lift** 5.7 (R/X)
E **Pebbles and Bam Bam** 5.10a (R)
F **Said and Done** 5.10b (?, ?)
G **Bruce Proof Roof** 5.11+ (?, ?)

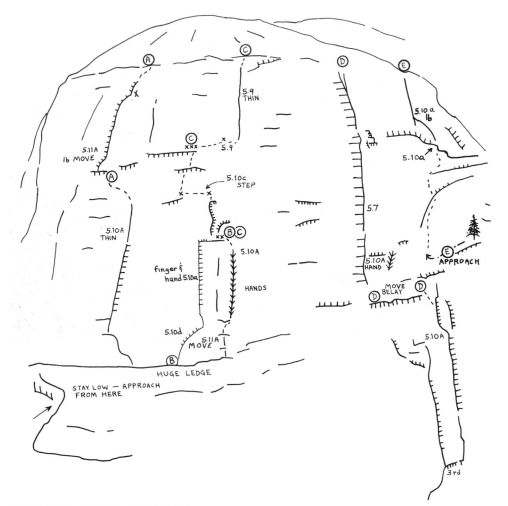

WEST COTTAGE DOME

The northwest face of this dome is approached from the Fairview Dome parking area and then heading up through the woods and across slabs to the notch between the east face of Daff Dome and West Cottage Dome. Drop down the slabby gully and continue right across slabs and small headwalls to the base.

A **Pencilitits** 5.11a pro: many small to 2½ inch (PG, ★)
B **Geekin' Hard** 5.10d (?, ?)
C **Pencil-Necked Geek** 5.10a (PG, ★)
D **Cottage Cheese** 5.10a (PG, ★)
E **Head Cheese** 5.10a (R)

Fist Fight 5.9 (?, ?) This climb is found on a small wall that is between West Cottage Dome and East Cottage Dome.

WEST COTTAGE DOME
1 Pencilitis
2 Pencil-necked Geek

3 Cottage Cheese
4 Head Cheese

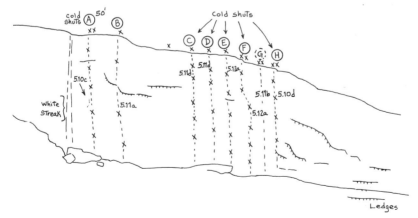

PEANUT GALLERY
A **Prognosis** 5.10c (PG, ★)
B **Plausible Deniability** 5.11a (R)
C **Diagnosis** 5.11d (PG, ★)
D **Trickanosis** 5.11d (PG, ★)

E **Osmosis** 5.12a (PG, ★)
F **Neurosis** 5.12a (PG, ★)
G **One-Armed Bandit** 5.11b (chopped) (★)
H **Platapus** 5.10d (PG, ★)

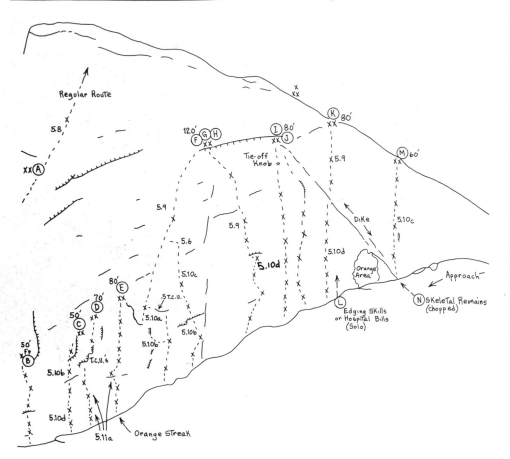

EAST COTTAGE DOME — WEST FACE

A multitude of fun face climbs are found on this west-facing dome. About 2.8 miles west of the Tuolumne Meadows Store on the north side of the road is a dirt turnout by a "slow traffic use turnouts" sign. From here hike up and slightly left over a small creek bed and then up to some slabs gaining the south (backside) summit of this dome. Stay high on the south side. **The Peanut Gallery** is the 60-foot cliff west and down below **Knobulator**.

A   **Regular Route** 5.8 (R)
B   **Flintstone** 5.10b (R, ★)
C   **The Bulge** 5.10d (PG, ★ ★)
D   **Liposuction** 5.11a (PG, ★)
E   **Orange Plasma** 5.11a (PG, ★)
F   **Ballroom Dancing** 5.10b (R/X)
G   **Comfortably Numb** 5.10c (R, ★ ★★)
H   **Old Folks Boogie** 5.10d (R, ★ ★)

I   **Knobvious** 5.10d (PG, ★ ★)
J   **Rover Take Over** 5.10d (PG, ★ ★)
K   **Knobnoxious** 5.10d (PG, ★ ★)
L   **Edging Skills or Hospital Bills** solo (X, ★)
M   **Knobulator** 5.10c (PG, ★)
N   **Skeletal Remains** (chopped) (X, ★)

EAST COTTAGE DOME
A   UPPER NORTH WALL
B   Spectra
C   PEANUT GALLERY
1   The Bulge
2   Orange Plazma
3   Knobvious
5   Knobulator

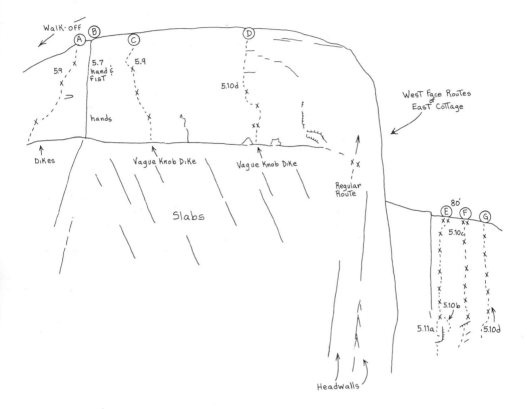

EAST COTTAGE DOME — UPPER & LOWER NORTH WALLS

APPROACH These climbs (A-D) are on a short wall at the top of the dome. Best approached from the east side coming down from the top of he dome. Climbs E-G are on a north-facing wall below **Flintstone**.

A **Two Left Shoes** 5.9 (R)
B **The Crack** 5.7 (PG, ★)
C **Late for Dinner Again** 5.9 (R)
D **Four-Finger Slooper** 5.10d (R)
E **Detente** 5.11a (?, ?)
F **Karin's Coming** 5.10c (?, ?)
G **Spectra** 5.10d (?, ?) #2 +#3 T.C.U.'s

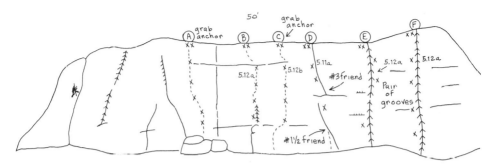

CANOPY WORLD — WEST FACE

Follow the Glen Aulin Trail for approximately three miles to the obvious dome, 150 yards to the right of the trail. When the river is low (mid-July on) the following approach is much shorter: Park at the western end of the meadows before Pothole Dome (small dome at west end of meadows). Skirt the dome on its eastern side until you reach the river. Go downstream for about 5 minutes until you see Canopy World on the other side.

A **Syncronicity** 5.12c (PG, ★)
B **Quantum Leap** 5.12a (PG, ★)
C **Realitivity** 5.12b (PG, ★)
D **Partners in Climb** 5.11a (PG, ★) 3 friend, 1½ friend
E **Go With The Flow** 5.12a (PG, ★) ¾ to 1½ T.C.U.'s
F **Spiro Gyro** 5.12a 5 bolts (PG, ★)

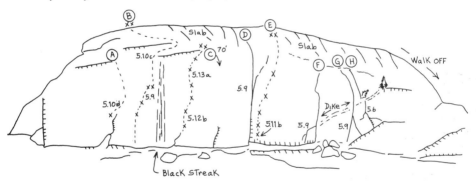

CANOPY WORLD — SOUTHWEST FACE

A **One-Eyed Jack** 5.10d (X)
B **Kill Pickle** 5.10c (R)
C **Sudden Impact** 5.13a (PG, ★)
D **Trick Shot** 5.9 (PG, ★)

E **Polski Wyrob** 5.11b (R, ★)
F **Billiard Room** 5.9 (PG, ★)
G **Kick Back Crack** 5.9 (PG)
H **Sweet 'n Low** 5.6 (PG)

CANOPY WORLD — NORTHEAST FACE

I **The Grapevine** 5.13a (PG, ★ ★ ★)
J **Top Pickle** 5.12a (PG/R, ★)

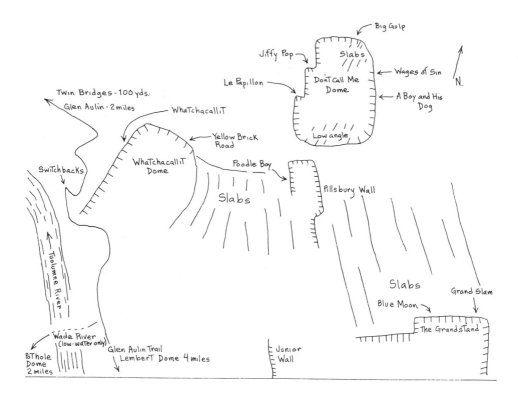

TWIN BRIDGES

Offering a multitude of varied short climbs and an escape from the hectic front country scene, Twin Bridges can be approached two ways. From the road that goes to the Tuloumne Meadows stables, follow the Glen Aulin trail for about four miles till you come to a point where there are some switchbacks and the river drops down on your left. On your right is Whatchacallit Dome. Follow this cliff down and right to the climbs **Poodle Boy**, etc. Continue your way around right to the Pillsbury Wall and the Grandstand, which is up high and right. A shorter but more complicated way is to park on the north side of the road about 2.6 miles west from the Tuolumne Meadows Store, just past Pothole Dome. Head north through the woods gaining a notch between Pothole Dome and a dome with erratics on your left. Drop through here to the river and cross to the other side or go further downstream to a footbridge which is past Whatchacallit Dome. The river crossing should be attempted only when the river is very low.

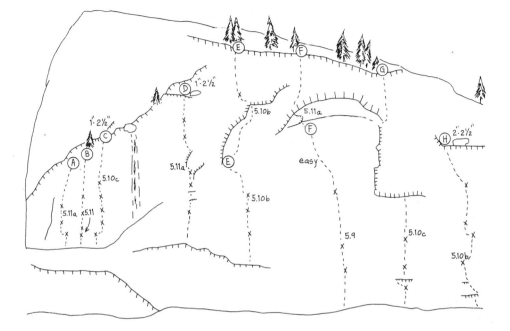

WHATCHACALLIT DOME — WEST FACE

A **Thigamajig** 5.11a (?, ?)
B **Whozamawhatsit** 5.11
C **Whatchacallit** 5.10c
D **Whatzisface** 5.11a
E **Crowd Pleaser** 5.10b
F **The Flapper** 5.11a
G **Gizmo** 5.10c
H **Skedaddle** 5.10b

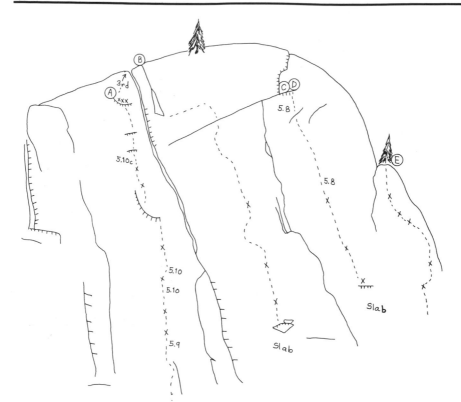

WHATCHACALLIT DOME – NORTH FACE

A **Yellow Brick Road** 5.10c
B **Ugly Face** 5.8
C **The Jogger** 5.7

D **A Walk in the Park** 5.8
E **The Wanderer** 5.9

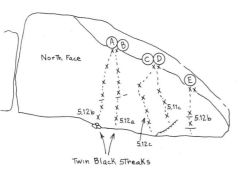

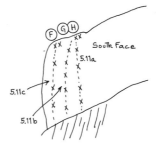

PILLSBURY DOME
– NORTH FACE

A **Icing** 5.12b (PG, ★ ★ ★)
B **Cupcake** 5.12a (PG, ★ ★ ★)
C **Patticake** 5.12c (PG, ★)
D **Susie Q** 5.11c (PG, ★)
E **Dough Boy** 5.12b (PG, ★)

PILLSBURY DOME
– SOUTH FACE

F **Black & White & Red All Over** 5.11c
G **A Man, A Boy, and His Poodle** 5.11b
H **Poodle Boy** 5.11a

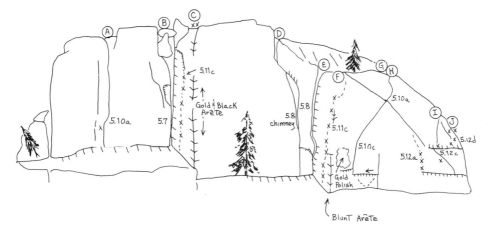

DON'T CALL ME DOME — SOUTH FACE

A **One Size Fits All** 5.10a (?, ?)
B **Grant's Gulch** 5.7 (PG)
C **Jiffy Pop** 5.11c (PG, ★ ★)
D **Charge Card** 5.8 (PG)
E **Big Business** 5.8 (PG)
F **Le Papillon** 5.11c (PG, ★ ★)

G **Fat Boys** 5.10c (PG, ★)
H **Cole Burner** 5.12a (R)
I **Party Bowl** 5.12c (PG, ★)
J **Perhaps, Another Bowl?** 5.12d (PG, ★ ★ ★) same start as **Party Bowl.**

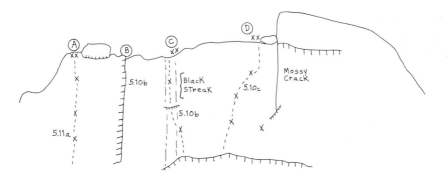

DON'T CALL ME DOME — WEST FACE

A **Big Gulp** 5.11a
B **Quick Stop** 5.10b

C **Two 4 The Price of One** 5.10b
D **Pit Stop** 5.10c

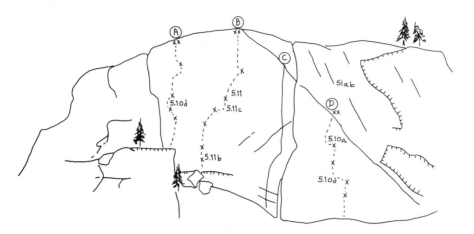

DONT CALL ME DOME — NORTH FACE

A **Man's Best Friend** 5.10d
B **A Boy and His Dog** 5.11c

C **Discount Crack** 5.9
D **Wages of Sin** 5.10d

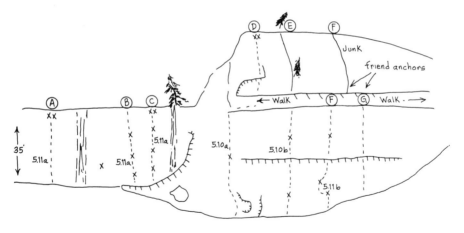

JUNIOR WALL

A **Rolo Solo** 5.11a (TR)
B **Slate Quarry** 5.11a
C **Mighty Mite** 5.11a

D **One for the Money** 5.10a
E **Two for the Money** 5.10b
F **Three to Get Ready** 5.11b
G **Go Cat Go** 5.10a (TR) solo

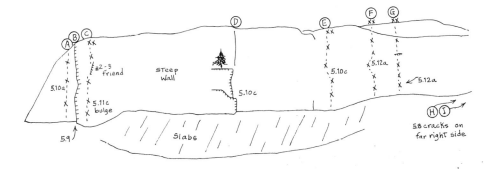

THE GRANDSTAND
A **Pop Fly** 5.10a
B **Becky's Corner** 5.9
C **Grand Slam** 5.11c
D **Ten A, My Ass** 5.10c
E **Spark Plug** 5.10c (PG, ★)
F **Blue Moon** 5.12a (PG, ★ ★)

G **Straight Away** 5.12a (?, ★ ★)
H **Sorry Dave** 5.8 (?, ?)
I **Snooze You Lose** 5.8 (?, ?)

LEMBERT DOME — WEST FACE
1   Lunar Leap
2   Double Stuff
3   Willie's Hand Jive
4   Rawl Drive
5   Truck n' Drive
6   Cucamonga Honey
7   The Water Cracks
8   Werner's Wiggle

LEMBERT DOME — NORTHWEST FACE

Approach from the parking area at the base of the west face. Go up and left along the base.

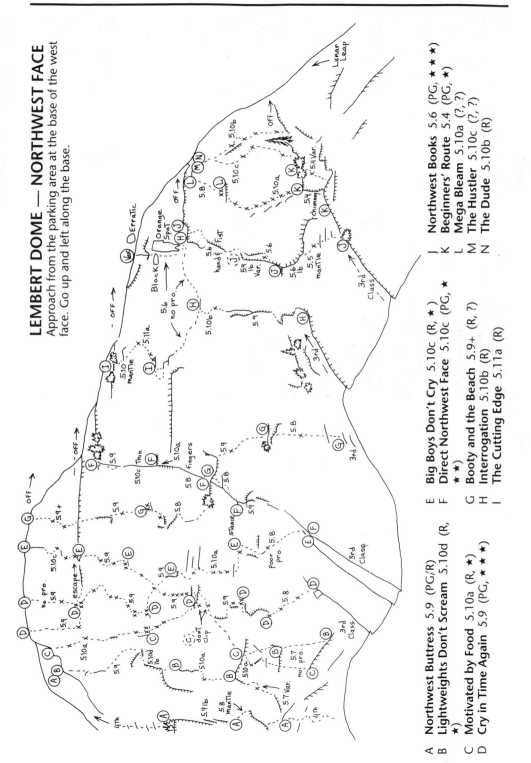

A   Northwest Buttress 5.9 (PG/R)
B   Lightweights Don't Scream 5.10d (R, ★)
C   Motivated by Food 5.10a (R, ★)
D   Cry in Time Again 5.9 (PG, ★ ★ ★)
E   Big Boys Don't Cry 5.10c (R, ★)
F   Direct Northwest Face 5.10c (PG, ★ ★)
G   Booty and the Beach 5.9+ (R, ?)
H   Interrogation 5.10b (R)
I   The Cutting Edge 5.11a (R)
J   Northwest Books 5.6 (PG, ★ ★ ★)
K   Beginners' Route 5.4 (PG, ★)
L   Mega Bleam 5.10a (?, ?)
M   The Hustler 5.10c (?, ?)
N   The Dude 5.10b (R)

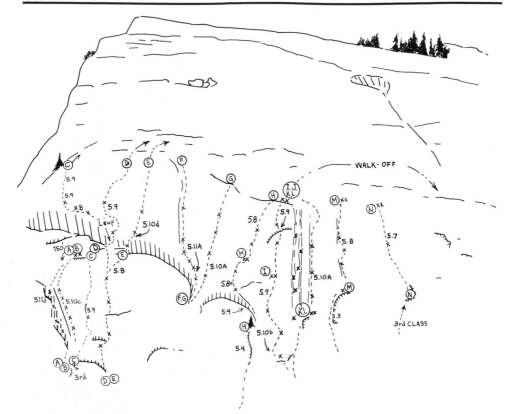

LEMBERT DOME — WEST FACE

This face lies just above the parking area on the north side of Hwy. 120, ¼ mile east of Tuolumne Meadows Campground.

A   **Never Give Up the Ship** 5.11d (R/X)
B   **Man Over Board** 5.10c (X to 1st bold, ★)
C   **Shoot the Moon** 5.9 (R/X, ?)
D   **Lunar Leap** 5.9 (R, ★)
E   **Double Stuff** 5.10d (R, ★)
F   **Willie's Hand Jive** 5.11a (R, ★)
G   **Rawl Drive** 5.10a (R/X)
H   **Truck n' Drive** 5.9 (R, ★ ★)
I   **Cucamonga Honey** 5.10b (R, ★)
J   **Left Water Crack** 5.7 (R, ★ ★)
K   **Right Water Crack** 5.8 (R, ★)
L   **Head Rush** 5.10a (R/X, ★)
M   **Werner's Wiggle** 5.8 (R, ★ ★)
N   **Blood Test** 5.7 (R/X)

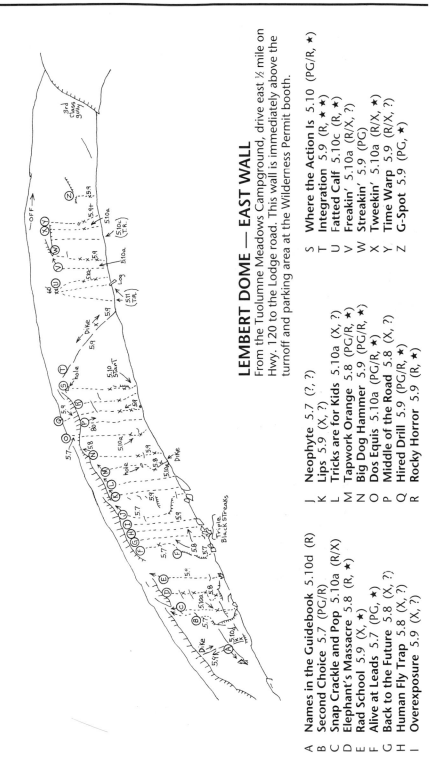

LEMBERT DOME — EAST WALL

From the Tuolumne Meadows Campground, drive east ½ mile on Hwy. 120 to the Lodge road. This wall is immediately above the turnoff and parking area at the Wilderness Permit booth.

A Names in the Guidebook 5.10d (R)
B Second Choice 5.7 (PG/R)
C Snap Crackle and Pop 5.10a (R/X)
D Elephant's Massacre 5.8 (R, ★)
E Rad School 5.9 (X, ★)
F Alive at Leads 5.7 (PG, ★)
G Back to the Future 5.8 (X, ?)
H Human Fly Trap 5.8 (X, ?)
I Overexposure 5.9 (X, ?)
J Neophyte 5.7 (?, ?)
K Lips 5.9 (X, ?)
L Tricks are for Kids 5.10a (X, ?)
M Tapwork Orange 5.8 (PG/R, ★)
N Big Dog Hammer 5.9 (PG/R, ★)
O Dos Equis 5.10a (PG/R, ★)
P Middle of the Road 5.8 (X, ?)
Q Hired Drill 5.9 (PG/R, ★)
R Rocky Horror 5.9 (R, ★)
S Where the Action Is 5.10 (PG/R, ★)
T Integration 5.9 (R, ★ ★)
U Fatted Calf 5.10c (R, ★)
V Freakin' 5.10a (R/X, ?)
W Streakin' 5.9 (PG)
X Tweekin' 5.10a (R/X, ★)
Y Time Warp 5.9 (R/X, ?)
Z G-Spot 5.9 (PG, ★)

DOG DOME

North Face 5.8   take the Dog Lake Trail from the trailhead located ½ mile east of Lembert Dome. Continue toward Young Lakes until the north face of Dog Dome can be seen from the meadow.

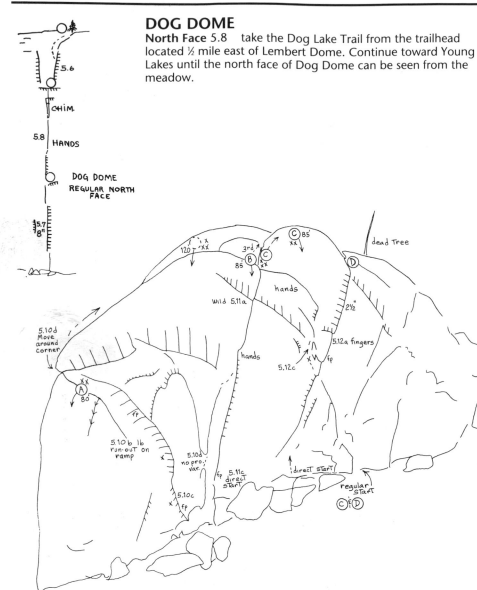

5.6

CHIM.

5.8 HANDS

DOG DOME
REGULAR NORTH
FACE

5.7
8"

dead Tree

3rd.
85
hands
wild 5.11a
2½"

5.10d
Move
around
corner

hands
5.12a fingers
5.12c
fp

A
80

5.10b 1b
run-out on
ramp
fp
5.10d
no pro.
var.
fp 5.11c
direct
start
direct start
regular
start
5.10c
x fp
C & D

PUPPY DOME

East of the Tuolumne Meadows Campground ½ mile is the turnoff for the Lodge. Puppy Dome is the small dome located just south of the Wilderness Permit booth and parking area. Walk around the west side of the dome, to the following south facing routes:

A   **Achilles** 5.10c (R)
B   **Do or Fly** 5.11c (PG, ★ ★ ★)   This is the left of two overhanging crack systems. There is a bolt anchor on top.
C   **Grenade Launcher** 5.12c (PG, ★ ★ ★)
D   **Horseshoes and Handgrenades** 5.12a pro: small to 3½ inch (PG, ★ ★ ★) This is the right slanting crack.

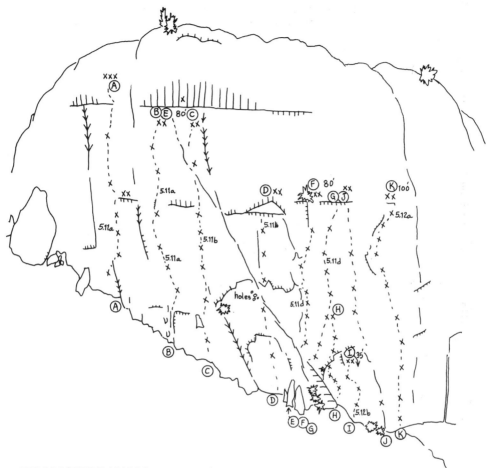

TRANSPIRE WALL

Go east on Hwy 120 until you come to the Tioga Pass entrance station. Three miles east of the station is Ellery Lake, with a dam at its eastern end. About one mile east of this dam (down the steep Lee Vining grade) is a large gray rock slide on the left side of the road. At the eastern end of slide is the beginning of a cliff band. These climbs are found where the slide area first meets the cliff and are just uphill and slightly left.

A **Mellow Yellow** 5.11a pro: 1-2, 2-2 friends (R, ★)
B **Harpole and the Hendersons** 5.11a pro: #4 rock + 2 friends (R, ★)
C **Rat Patrol** 5.11b (PG)
D **Walk Like An Egyptian** 5.11b pro: 2 1/2 (PG, ★)
E **Transpire Crack** 5.10a (PG)
F **Scratch 'n Sniff** 5.11d pro: ¾ to 2 (PG, ★ ★)
G **Itchy Scratchy** 5.11d pro: 2½ friends (PG, ★ ★)
H **Red Don't Go** 5.12b (PG, ★ ★)
    Stickie Wickiet 5.12a (PG, ★) Variation to H — climb up ramp left, then traverse back right past 1 bolt into the roof on **Red Don't Go**.
I **Wicked Stiffy** 5.12b (PG, ★ ★)
J **Fuel Pump** 5.10d pro: to 3 inch (R)
K **Wicked Itchy** 5.12a (★ ★, R/short people)

MT. CONNESS — SOUTHWEST FACE

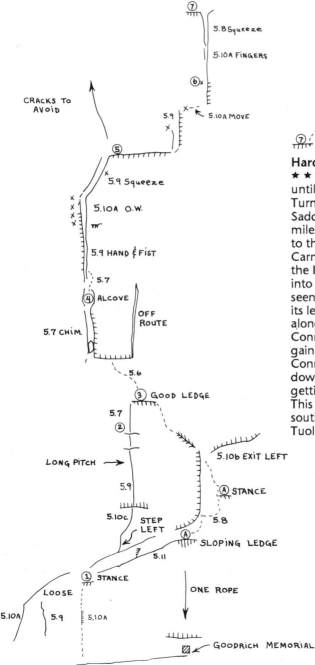

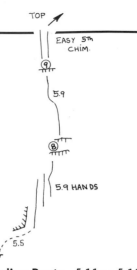

CRACKS TO AVOID

⑦ 5.8 Squeeze

5.10A FINGERS

⑥ x — 5.10A MOVE

5.9 x — 5.10A MOVE

⑤ 5.9 Squeeze

5.10A O.W.

5.9 HAND & FIST

5.7

④ ALCOVE

OFF ROUTE

5.7 CHIM

5.6

③ GOOD LEDGE

5.7

②

LONG PITCH →

5.9

5.10c STEP LEFT

5.8

Ⓐ SLOPING LEDGE

5.11

① STANCE

LOOSE

5.10A 5.9 5.10A

TOP

EASY 5th CHIM.

⑨

5.9

⑧

5.9 HANDS

⑦ 5.5

5.10b EXIT LEFT

Ⓐ STANCE

ONE ROPE

GOODRICH MEMORIAL

Harding Route 5.11 or 5.10c (PG, ★ ★ ★) Drive east on Hwy 120 until two miles east of Tioga Pass. Turn left onto the road that leads to Saddlebag Lake. After about 1½ miles a blocked off road will be seen to the left which leads to the Carnegie Institute. Follow this past the Institute and up along a stream into the canyon. A large rock cliff seen ahead is passed via a notch on its left side. Now head up right along the east shoulder of Mt. Conness until the plateau above is gained. When the summit of Mt. Conness can be seen ahead drop down a gully to the west before getting too close to the summit. This will lead to the base of the southwest face. Refer to the USGS Tuolumne Meadows Quadrangle.

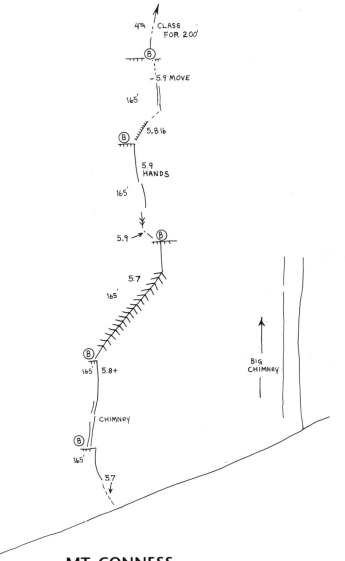

MT. CONNESS

Morning Thunder 5.9 (PG/R, ★)   This route is located about ½ mile east of the **Harding Route** and just left of a huge, deep chimney system. Approach as for the **Harding Route**.

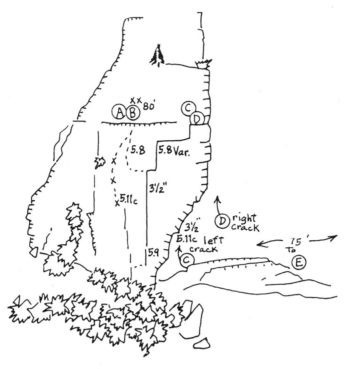

PRIVATE PROPERTY

Climbing unlike that of Tuolumne with some excellent multipitch cracks and some way pro-d sport climbs. Park in a turnout on the right with a camera sign .8 mile east of the Ellery Lake Dam. Drop down off the road onto a quite steep and loose hillside with some third class and follow the cliff down right for about 10 minutes. Ellerry Lake is about 3 miles east of the Tioga Pass entrance station.

A **Executive Decision** 5.11c pro: small 2 wires (R, ★)
B **Quaking Aspen** 5.9 (PG, ★ ★)
C **Double Cream, Double Sugar** 5.11c pro: 3-3, 3-3½, 3-4 (PG, ★)
D **Ferd's Follies** 5.10d (?)
Radar Detector 5.12a Down and left several hundred feet from **Executive Decision** one will see a 150-foot wall with a tower on top of it. This 2-pitch route ascends the middle of the wall.

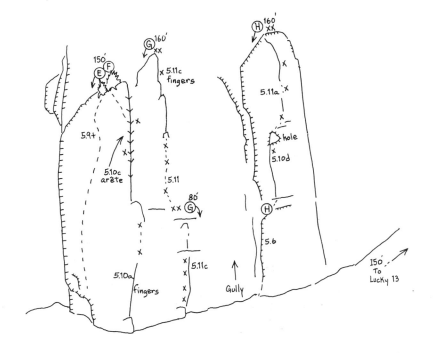

THE GOLD WALL

E   **Gold Wall** 5.9+ (?, ?)
F   **Tastes Great** 5.10c (?, ?)
G   **Less Filling** 5.11c (PG, ★)
H   **Hole in the Wall** 5.11a (?, ?)

PRIVATE PROPERTY

A **Lucky 13** 5.10d pro: wired T.C.U.'s (R)
B **Torqued** 5.11b (PG, ★)
C **Made for the Shade** 5.11c (5.12a var.) (R, ?)
D **Falk's Folly** 5.10a (R)
E **Iya** 5.12b pro: ½ to 2½ (PG, ★ ★) To reduce rope drag, use two-rope technique to get to the first bolt.
F **Spike** 5.12c (PG, ★ ★)
G **Invader** 5.10a (PG, ★)
H **Get to the Roof** 5.11b pro: 1½ -2 friends (R, ?)
I **Dangle Fest** 5.12c pro: 2-3, 3-3½, 3-4 draws (PG, ★ ★)
J **Jawbone Jitterbug** 5.11c pro: to 2½ inch (?)
K **Earshot** 5.12c pro: stoppers T.C.U.'s (?, ?)
L **Titslinger** 5.11c pro: to 2½ inch (R, ★)

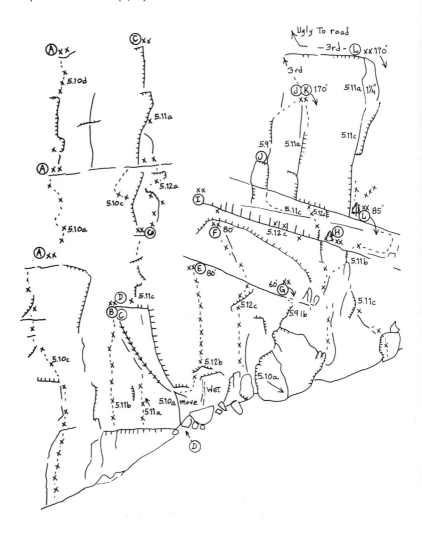

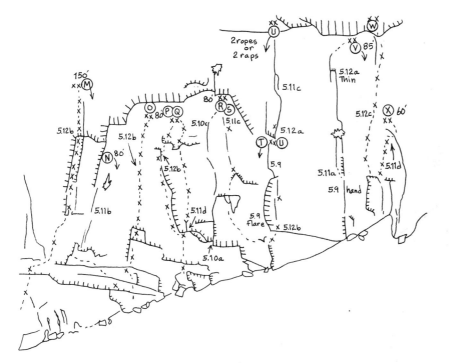

PRIVATE PROPERTY
M **Silver Bullet** 5.12b (PG, ★ ★ ★)
N **Dynomike** 5.11b (R)
O **Felix** 5.12b (PG, ★ ★)
P **Master Cylinder** 5.12b (PG, ★ ★ ★)
Q **Bag 'o Tricks** 5.11d (PG, ★ ★)
R **Golden Eagle** 5.10c (R)
S **Coq Au Vin** 5.11c (?, ?)
T **Stalag 13** 5.9 (?, ?)
U **Mean Left** 5.12a (R, ★)
V **Stones Throw** 5.12a pro: thin stoppers 2½ inch (PG, ★ ★)
W **The Finger** 5.12c (PG, ★ ★)
X **Poindexter** 5.11d (PG, ★ ★)

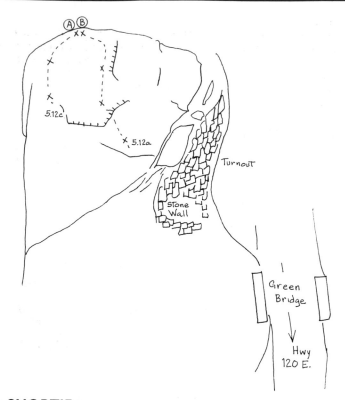

WICKED SHORTIE

APPROACH These climbs are on a small cliff ½ mile east of the Ellery Lake Dam. Park in a large turnout on the right just before a green bridge. Look over the wall at this small cliff 30 seconds off the road.

A **Xtra** 5.12c (R, ★ ★)
B **Wicked Shortie** 5.12a (PG, ★ ★)

GREEN BRIDGE

These climbs are on a 65-foot cliff on the right side of the gully that is below the green bridge (**Wicked Shortie** approach). It can be approached by either going back uphill past the Wicked Shortie, then dropping down and coming back around below the cliff. One can also climb down the third class on the downhill side of the bridge.

(Left) **EZ Duz It** 5.12a (PG, ★ ★ ★)

(Right) **We Want EZ** 5.12b (PG, ★ ★ ★)

ELLERY LAKE T.R. AREA

A short little lead and some top ropes are found here. Park at the Ellery Lake Dam and then gain an old mining road on the other side. Follow this downhill for about 10 minutes.

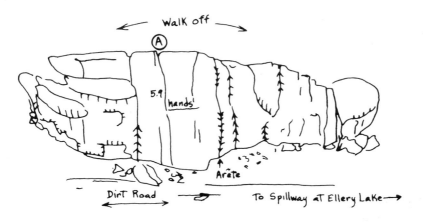

SPILLWAY CRAG

A   **Gold Mind** 5.9 (PG, ★)

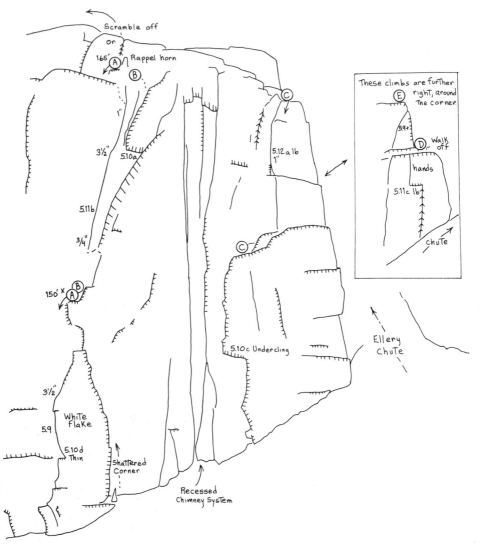

SPEED OF LIFE

APPROACH The bowl above Ellery Lake is home for this high quality crack route and several other climbs. Drive east on Hwy. 120 until about three miles past Tioga Pass Entrance Station and park at a dam at the eastern end of Ellery Lake. These climbs are up on **Golden Rock** on the west side of the bowl, left of a long, narrow gully, about 1/2 mile from the road.

A **Speed of Life** 5.11b pro: small to 3½ inch, esp. ¾-1¼ (PG, ★ ★ ★)
B **Moose and Squirrell** 5.10a (?, ?)
C **Codex** 5.12a (?, ?)
D **Moon Dawg** 5.9+ (?, ?)
E **Full Speed Ahead** 5.11c (?, ?)

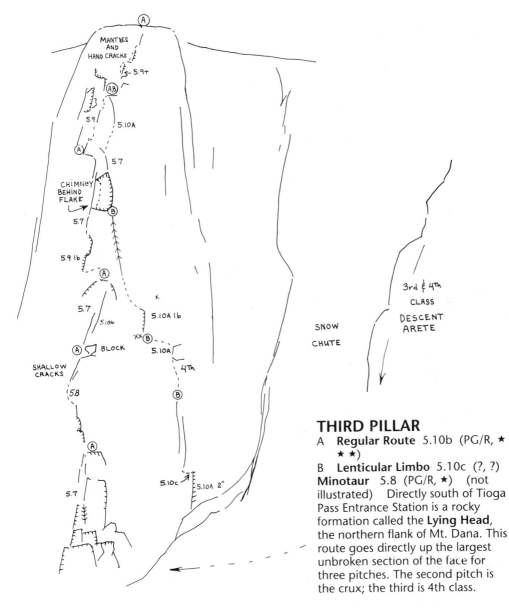

THIRD PILLAR

A **Regular Route** 5.10b (PG/R, ★ ★ ★)

B **Lenticular Limbo** 5.10c (?, ?)
Minotaur 5.8 (PG/R, ★) (not illustrated) Directly south of Tioga Pass Entrance Station is a rocky formation called the **Lying Head**, the northern flank of Mt. Dana. This route goes directly up the largest unbroken section of the face for three pitches. The second pitch is the crux; the third is 4th class.

APPROACH Park in a paved turnout ½ mile east of Tioga Pass, at the western end of Tioga Lake. High to the east of can be seen the edge of the Dana Plateau. This wonderful route remains hidden on that edge, overlooking the east. The climb is best approached by going past the west end of Tioga Lake and up toward the canyon between the Dana Plateau and Mt. Dana. Once in the mouth of the canyon travel diagonally up left through a talus field to gain the Dana Plateau. Move over to the eastern edge of the Plateau where a view of Mono Lake can be seen, as well as the top of a prominent angular pillar that juts off to the east. This is the **Third Pillar**. Just north of the pillar is a snow filled couloir with an Arête just to the left. Descend down this Arête via 3rd and 4th class climbing.

CATHEDRAL PEAK

Southeast Buttress 5.6 (PG, ★ ★ ★) (not illustrated) Park at the Cathedral Lakes trailhead (1¾ miles west of Tuolumne Meadows Campground) and follow the trail up to Budd Lake. This trail is unmarked and cuts off left toward Budd Creek 1/4 mile up the Cathedral Lakes Trail. Before reaching Budd Lake hike up and right toward the prominent buttress seen ahead. Numerous 5th class routes are possible up this cliff. The most popular starts 150 feet up and right from the toe of the buttress. Most of the routes converge into a short prominent chimney halfway up. Three more pitches of better climbing follow flakes and cracks to the top.

EICHORN PINNACLE

A **West Pillar** (PG/R, ★ ★) This is the prominent buttress which rises above Upper Cathedral Lake, on the west side of Cathedral Peak. To approach, park at Cathedral Lakes trailhead and follow the Sunrise/Cathedral Lakes trail for approximately three miles. This climb will be seen up above slabs that overlook the lake. As an alternative approach, hike as to the Southeast Buttress, but continue to follow the base of the wall west.

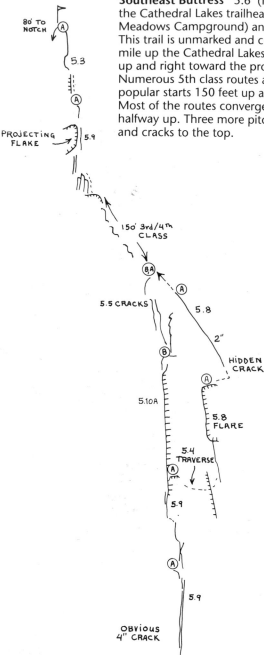

MARMOT DOME

Park in a paved turnout at the western end of Tuolumne Meadows, directly across from Pothole Dome. Southwest from this point, Marmot Dome presents a strikingly beautiful polished ramp which crosses its midsection.

1	Scratch	4	Holiday on Rock
2	Mop and Glow	5	Easy Day
3	Slabstick		

Quickie 5.7 (?, ?) This route ascends the open slabs on the right side of Marmot Dome. Start left of a dirty, right facing, slanting corner and climb past three small overhangs to a belay atop a right facing open book. An easy pitch leads up and left to a broken ledge. The third pitch ascends the smooth, low angle face above (5.4).

Obscure Destiny 5.11 (R) This route lies just left of the vague break between Marmot Dome and the wall to the west that joins to Fariview Dome. Starting from the highest trees, on a ledge which slants up and left, climb two right facing corners to a block. Climb past a bolt, and the crux, to a second bolt. Continue first up and left, then up and right to a fixed pin. Move straight left, then back up and right to a horizontal crack. A difficult mantle and face climbing leads past a third bolt to a stance with two pins. One more easier pitch leads to the top. To descend, work down and right over tree covered ledges to a short rappel.

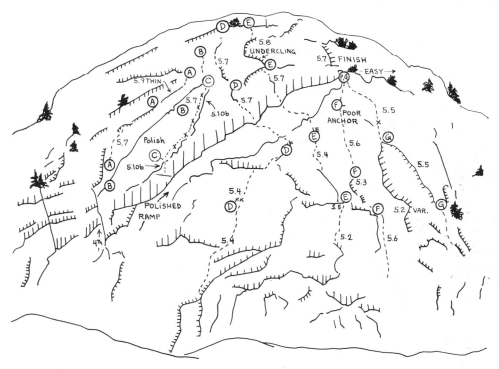

MARMOT DOME

A **Mop and Glow** 5.9 (PG)
B **Scratch** 5.7 (PG/R, ★)
C **Mother Lode** 5.10b (R, ★)
D **Slabstick** 5.7 (R, ★)

E **Holiday on Rock** 5.8 (PG/R, ★)
F **Low Pro** 5.6 (R/X)
G **Easy Day** 5.5 (R, ★)

RAZOR BACK

These routes lie on the wall that is between Marmot Dome and Fairview Dome; this wall terminates into the northeastern side of Fairview Dome.

Offday 5.9 (R) Start this route a few hundred feet right of the break in the wall between Marmot Dome and these cliffs that connect to Fairview. Ascend the polished apron to a left facing dihedral. Turn an arch on its right and face climb to a ledge with trees. Continue up the poorly protected and lichen covered rock above.

Juvenile Delinquent 5.8 (R) Begin the route a short distance right of **Offday** and climb up the face to a perched block. Step left and climb past a bolt to a scooped out ledge. Climb up and left over blocks to a long ledge and bush belay. An easier but poorly protected pitch leads to the top.

First Verse 5.10d (R, ?) This route is located a few hundred feet right of **Juvenile Delinquent**. Face climb past two bolts (5.10c) to a belay, then past three more bolts (5.10d) to a second belay at a tree. Climb a 5.7 corner above to the top. Descend with three 150 foot rappels off trees to the right.

Pot Luck 5.11a (TR) This is an overhanging hand crack located on the west side of Pothole Dome. Park in the large paved turnout across from Marmot Dome and hike around the west (left) side for about a quarter mile.

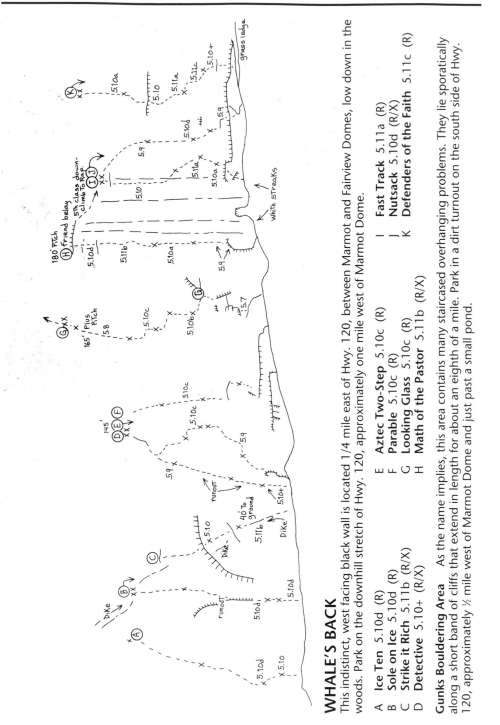

WHALE'S BACK

This indistinct, west facing black wall is located 1/4 mile east of Hwy. 120, between Marmot and Fairview Domes, low down in the woods. Park on the downhill stretch of Hwy. 120, approximately one mile west of Marmot Dome.

A **Ice Ten** 5.10d (R)
B **Sole on Ice** 5.10d (R)
C **Strike it Rich** 5.11b (R/X)
D **Detective** 5.10+ (R/X)

E **Aztec Two-Step** 5.10c (R)
F **Parable** 5.10c (R)
G **Looking Glass** 5.10c (R)
H **Math of the Pastor** 5.11b (R/X)

I **Fast Track** 5.11a (R)
J **Nutsack** 5.10d (R/X)
K **Defenders of the Faith** 5.11c (R)

Gunks Bouldering Area   As the name implies, this area contains many staircased overhanging problems. They lie sporadically along a short band of cliffs that extend in length for about an eighth of a mile. Park in a dirt turnout on the south side of Hwy. 120, approximately ½ mile west of Marmot Dome and just past a small pond.

FAIRVIEW DOME

This is the largest Dome in Tuolumne Meadows and the Regular Route is listed in the *Fifty Classic Climbs of North America*. Gads of multipitch climbs, all of excellent quality, adorn this sought after rock, but don't get caught on the face in an afternoon thunder storm. Located about 3.3 miles west of the Tuolumne Meadows Store and across form Daff Dome, park in the obvious turnout on the south side of the road.

1	Burning Down the House	5	Pièce de Résistance
2	Inverted Staircase	6	Heart of Stone
3	Regular Route	7	Lucky Streaks
4	Plastic Exploding Inevitable	8	Unh-Huh

DESCENT   Descend all the routes of Fairview by hiking down slabs on the south side before moving around to the west.

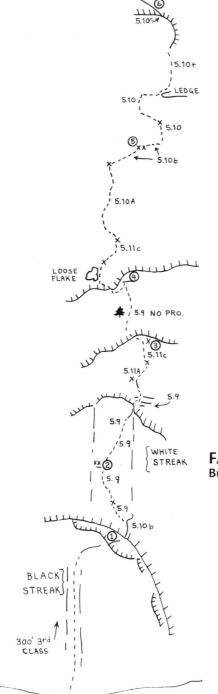

FAIRVIEW DOME — LEFT SIDE
Burning Down the House 5.11c (X, ★)

FAIRVIEW DOME — LEFT SIDE
Inverted Staircase 5.10b (PG/R, ★)

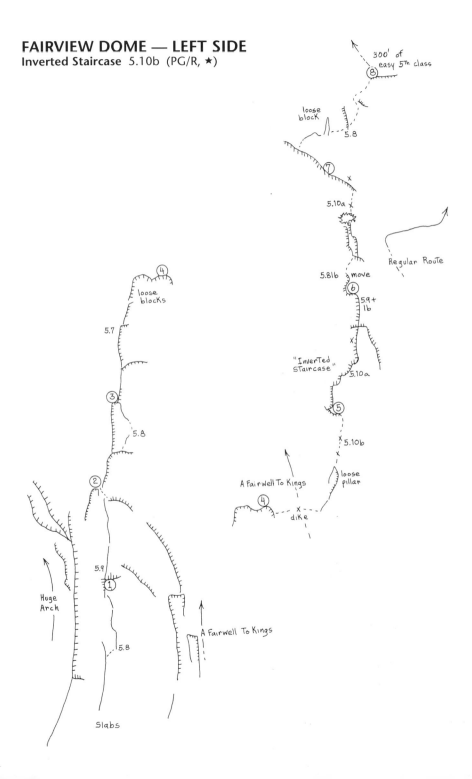

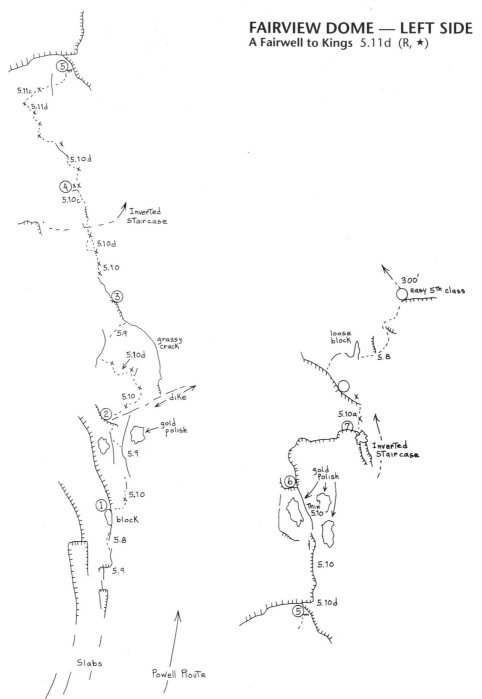

FAIRVIEW DOME — LEFT SIDE
A Fairwell to Kings 5.11d (R, ★)

FAIRVIEW DOME

A **Powell Route** 5.9 (PG)
B **Fairest of "Al"** 5.10d (PG/R, ★)
C **Regular Route** 5.9 (PG, ★ ★ ★)
D **Fiddler on the Roof** 5.10a pro: many runners (R, ?)
E **Inevitable Conclusions** 5.11b (PG/R, ★)
F **Wonderful Wino** 5.10b (?, ?)
DESCENT   Descend all the routes of Fairview by hiking down slabs on the south side before moving around to the west.

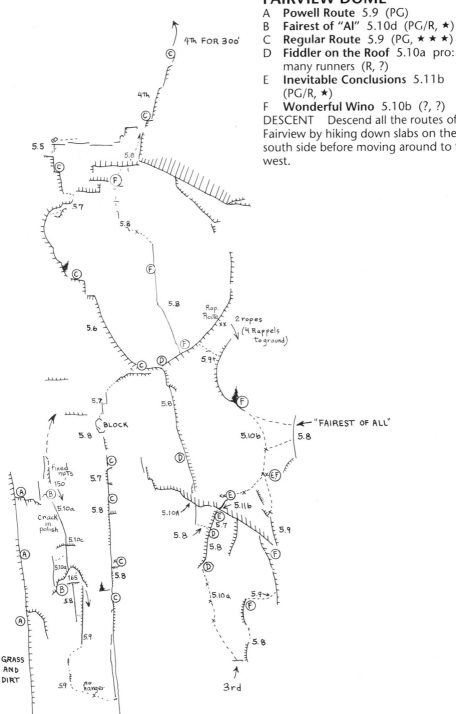

4th FOR 300'

4th

5.5

5.8

.57

5.7

5.8

5.8

Rap. Route
XX 2 ropes
(4 Rappels to ground)

5.6

5.9+

5.7

5.8

BLOCK

5.8

"FAIREST OF ALL"

5.10b   5.8

fixed nuts
150'

5.7

Crack in polish

5.10a

5.8

5.10A

5.10c

5.11b

5.7

5.8

5.9

5.10a

165

5.8

5.8

5.8

5.8

5.10a   5.9→

5.9

GRASS AND DIRT

5.9   no hanger

3rd

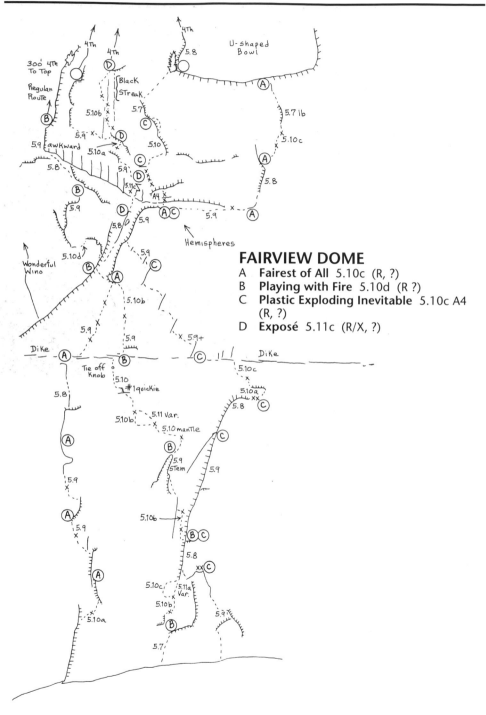

FAIRVIEW DOME

A **Fairest of All** 5.10c (R, ?)
B **Playing with Fire** 5.10d (R ?)
C **Plastic Exploding Inevitable** 5.10c A4
    (R, ?)
D **Exposé** 5.11c (R/X, ?)

FAIRVIEW DOME – WEST FACE
1 Plastic Exploding Inevitable
2 Pièce de Résistance
3 Heart of Stone
4 Mr. Kamps
5 Lucky Streaks
6 Unh-Huh
7 Great Pumpkin
8 Magical Mystery Tour

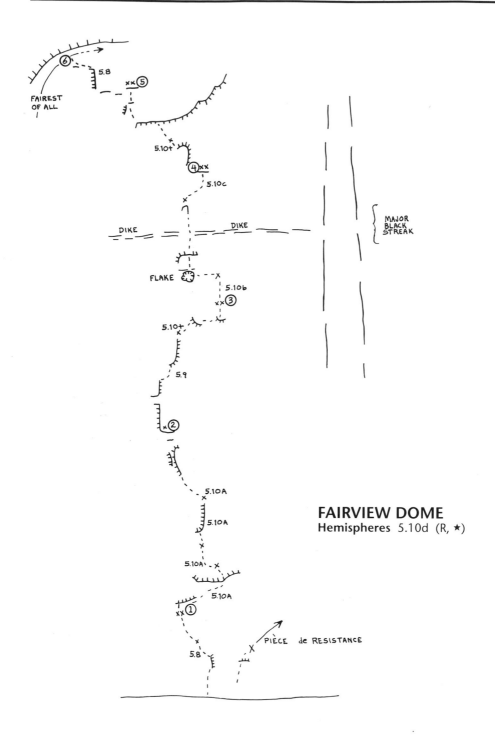

5.8

xx ⑤

FAIREST
OF ALL

5.10⁺

④ xx

5.10c

DIKE ——— DIKE

MAJOR
BLACK
STREAK

FLAKE x

5.10b

xx ③

5.10⁺

5.9

x ②

5.10A

5.10A

5.10A x

5.10A

xx ①

PIÈCE de RESISTANCE

5.8

FAIRVIEW DOME
Hemispheres 5.10d (R, ★)

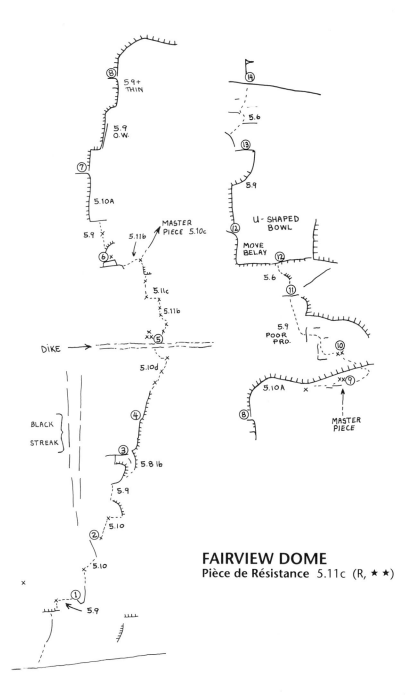

FAIRVIEW DOME
Pièce de Résistance 5.11c (R, ★ ★)

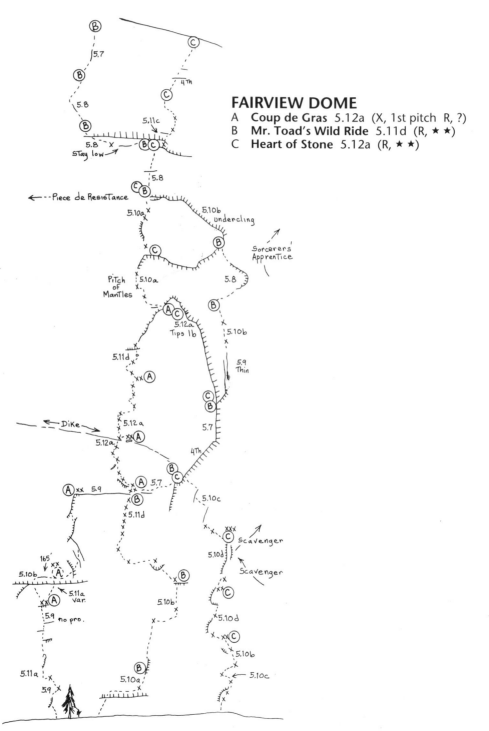

FAIRVIEW DOME
A **Coup de Gras** 5.12a (X, 1st pitch R, ?)
B **Mr. Toad's Wild Ride** 5.11d (R, ★ ★)
C **Heart of Stone** 5.12a (R, ★ ★)

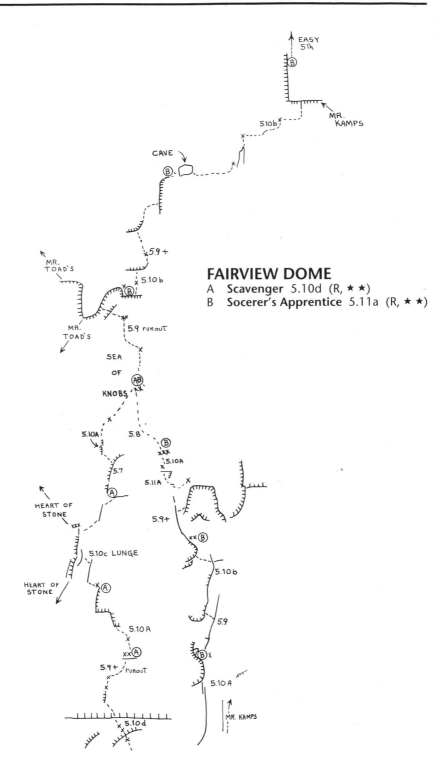

FAIRVIEW DOME
A **Scavenger** 5.10d (R, ★ ★)
B **Socerer's Apprentice** 5.11a (R, ★ ★)

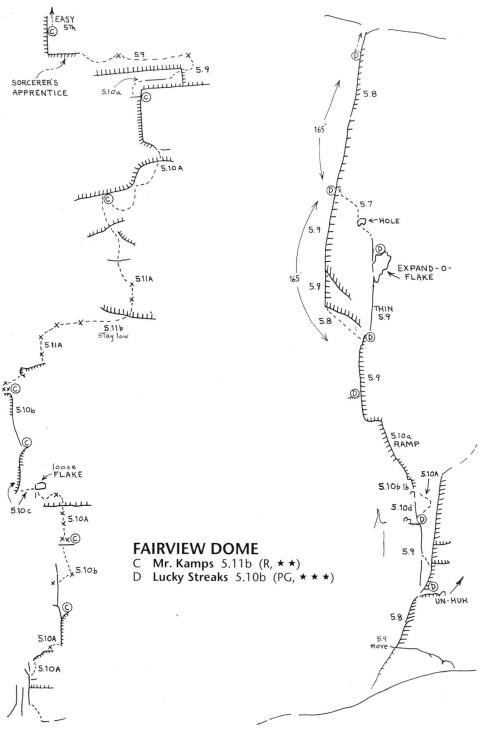

FAIRVIEW DOME
C **Mr. Kamps** 5.11b (R, ★★)
D **Lucky Streaks** 5.10b (PG, ★★★)

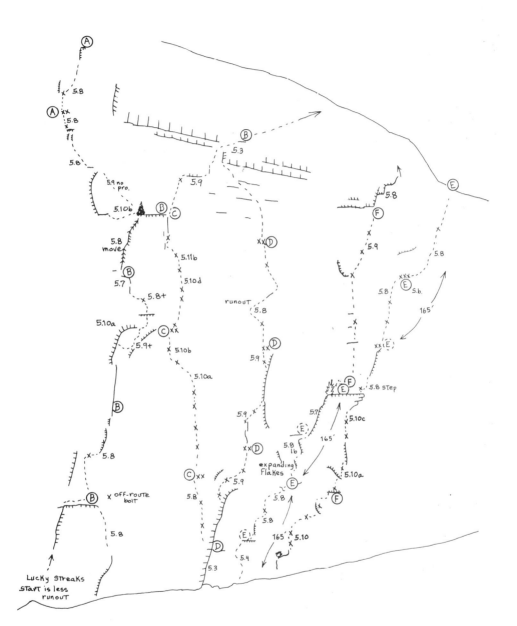

FAIRVIEW DOME — RIGHT SIDE

A **Unh-Unh** 5.10b (?, ?)
B **Unh-Huh** 5.10a pro: many small to 2½ inch (R, ★)
C **La Bella Luna** 5.11b (?, ?)
D **Roseanne** 5.9 pro: nuts to 2½ inch (R, ★ ★)
E **Great Pumpkin** 5.8 (PG/R, ★ ★)
F **When You're Strange** 5.10c (?, ?)

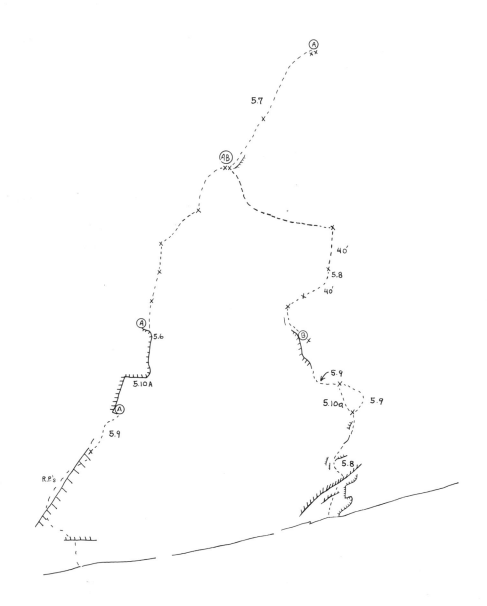

FAIRVIEW DOME
A   **Peter, Peter** 5.10a (R, ★)
B   **King Midas** 5.9 (R, ★)

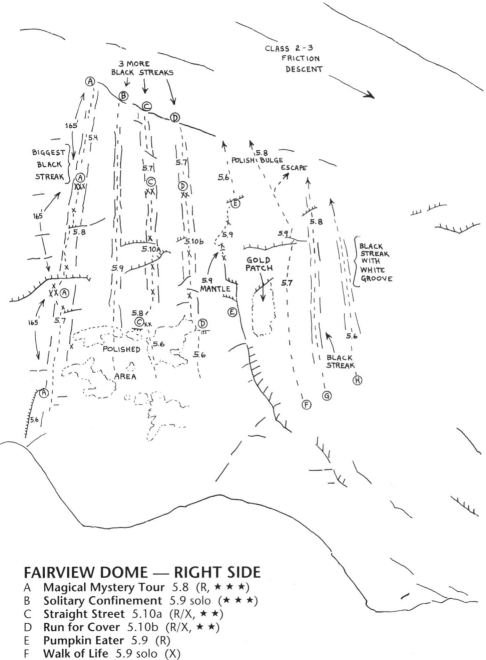

FAIRVIEW DOME — RIGHT SIDE

A   **Magical Mystery Tour** 5.8 (R, ★ ★ ★)
B   **Solitary Confinement** 5.9 solo (★ ★ ★)
C   **Straight Street** 5.10a (R/X, ★ ★)
D   **Run for Cover** 5.10b (R/X, ★ ★)
E   **Pumpkin Eater** 5.9 (R)
F   **Walk of Life** 5.9 solo (X)
G   **Blue Moon** 5.8 solo (X)
H   **Silverado** 5.6 solo (X)

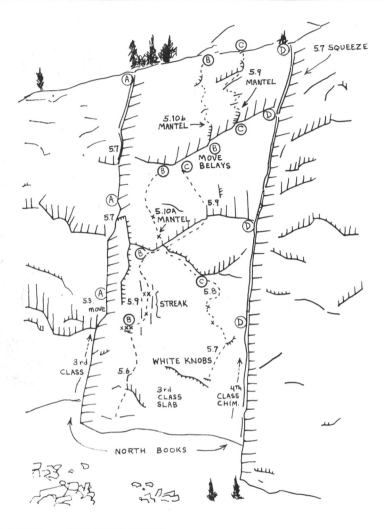

THE LAMB — NORTH FACE

On the eastern end of Lamb Dome are two long and deep chimney/offwidth cracks
(**North Books**). Goblin Girl and **Green Goblin** lie on the face between the two cracks.

A **Left North Book** 5.7 (PG/R, ★)
B **Goblin Girl** 5.10b (R, ★)
C **Green Goblin** 5.9 (R, ★)
D **Right North Book** 5.7 (PG/R, ★)

Birthday Party 5.8 (?, ?) Start about 150 feet left of **North Books** and follow a dike
system for about three or four pitches. Near the top work up and right through 5.8
headwalls and an unprotected 5.7 slab.

Black Sheep 5.8 (?, ?) Start about 500 feet left of the **North Books** and climb up, then
right through a bulge to a belay at a piton. The next headwall is climbed on the right
wall of a corner, past two pins. Above, an unprotected slab (about 40 feet right of
Birthday Party) leads to easier climbing.

THE LAMB – North

1 North Book
2 Goblin Girl
3 Green Goblin
4 Right North Book

5 Passover
6 Left Corner
7 Right Crack
8 Jog Corner

Passover 5.9 (R) This route is just right of the **North Books** and left of a thin crack (**Left Crack**). Wander up the face to just below some roofs. Pitch two goes up through a couple small roofs. The last pitch continues up past one more roof and onto slabs that lead to the top.

Left Crack 5.8 (PG/R) This is the left of two thin cracks on the face right of **Passover**. Lieback up a steep corner to a small ledge. The second pitch involves complicated climbing that leads to a pitch of 4th class and the top.

Right Crack 5.9 (PG/R) This is the other thin crack. The first pitch leads to a 3 inch (crux) crack. Pitch two is easier and leads to simple scrambling.

Job Corner 5.7 This climb ascends the very large left facing corner that is to right of **Right Crack**. Towards the top there are two possible escapes.

THE LAMB — WEST FACE

Park in the dirt turnout on the south side of the road about 4.7 miles west from the Tuolumne Meadows Store. Same parking area for Drug Dome.

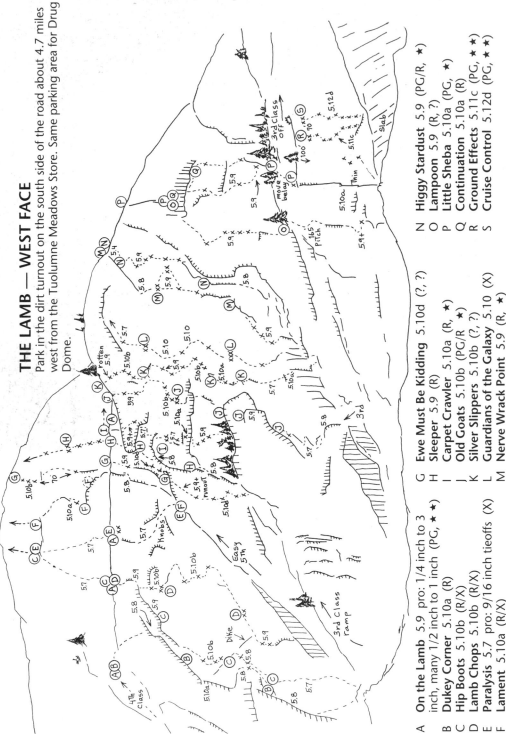

A **On the Lamb** 5.9 pro: 1/4 inch to 3 inch, many 1/2 inch to 1 inch (PG, ★ ★)
B **Dukey Corner** 5.10a (R)
C **Hip Boots** 5.10b (R/X)
D **Lamb Chops** 5.10b (R/X)
E **Paralysis** 5.7 pro: 9/16 inch tieoffs (X)
F **Lament** 5.10a (R/X)

G **Ewe Must Be Kidding** 5.10d (?, ?)
H **Sleeper** 5.9 (R)
I **Carpet Crawler** 5.10a (R, ★)
J **Old Goats** 5.10b (PG/R ★)
K **Silver Slippers** 5.10b (?, ?)
L **Guardians of the Galaxy** 5.10 (X)
M **Nerve Wrack Point** 5.9 (R, ★)

N **Higgy Stardust** 5.9 (PG/R, ★)
O **Lampoon** 5.9 (R, ?)
P **Little Sheba** 5.10a (PG, ★)
Q **Continuation** 5.10a (R)
R **Ground Effects** 5.11c (PG, ★ ★)
S **Cruise Control** 5.12d (PG, ★ ★)

DRUG DOME
1 Oz
2 Gram Traverse
3 Sunshine
4 Lord of the Overhigh
5 Dragonfly

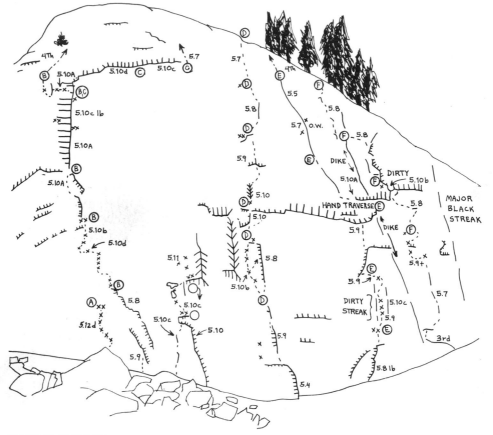

DRUG DOME

Park west of Lamb Dome about 4.7 miles west of Tuolumne Meadows Store and hike up and across the lower end of its western shoulder. From here, Drug Dome can be recognized by the distinctive roof near its summit.

A   **Ice** 5.12d (PG, ★ ★)
B   **Oz** 5.10d pro: small to 3 inch, esp. 1½-2 inch (PG, ★ ★ ★)
C   **Gram Traverse** 5.10d (PG/R, ★ ★)
D   **Sunshine** 5.10b (R, ★ ★)
E   **Lord of the Overhigh** 5.10c (R)
F   **Dragonfly** 5.10b (R)

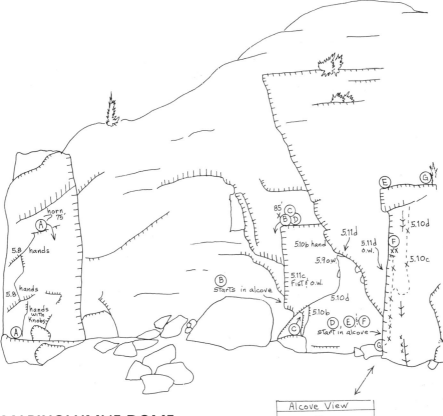

MARIUOLUMNE DOME — NORTH WALL

Approach as for Drug Dome, from the west end of Lamb Dome. Skirt the east side of Drug Dome before heading back right to talus and slabs that lead to the north wall.

A **Seconds to Darkness** 5.8 (PG, ★)
B **Easy Wind** 5.11c pro: 3½ inch- 6 inch, esp. 4 inch-5 inch (PG, ★ ★)
C **Arms Race** 5.10d pro: small to 3½ inch, esp. 1 inch-2 inch, one 5 inch (PG, ★ ★ ★)
D **Hysteria** 5.11d (PG, ★ ★ ★)
E **Missing Link** 5.11c pro: many 4 inch-6 inch (PG, ★ ★)
F **Stubble Face** 5.12b (?, ?)
G **Razor Back** 5.10d (PG/R, ★ ★ ★)

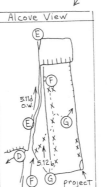

Alcove View

MARIUOLUMNE DOME
1 Stomper
2 Strider
3 Middle Earth
4 Hobbit Book
5 Mesmerized
6 The Cony
7 Galadriel
8 Sharky's End
9 The Nazgul

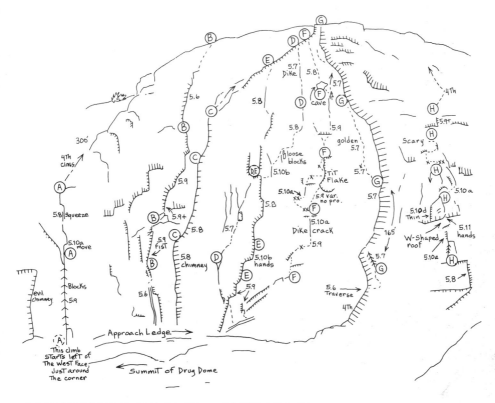

MARIUOLUMNE DOME — WEST FACE

Park at the west end of Lamb Dome and hike up to and around the eastern end of Drug Dome. From that dome's summit, continue west on ledges to the base of the wall. A bolted 4-pitch route exists that is just down and left from the **Hobbit Book.** It can be used to approach climbs **Stomper** through **Mesmerized.** There is a semi unprotected 5.8 mantle out left on the 4th pitch or one can follow the last bolts at 5.11.

A **Shrouds Have No Pockets** 5.8 (PG, ★)
B **Stomper** 5.9+ (PG, ★)
C **Strider** 5.8 (PG)
D **Whalin' Dwalin** 5.10b (?, ?)

E **Serrated Edge** 5.10b (PG, ★ ★)
F **Middle Earth** 5.10a (PG, ★ ★)
G **Hobbit Book** 5.7 (R, ★ ★ ★)
H **Mesmerized** 5.11 (R, ★)

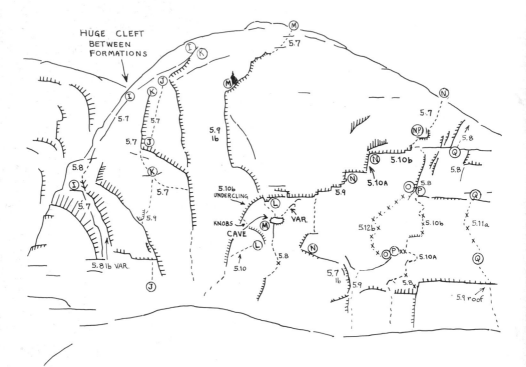

MARIUOLUMNE DOME — RIGHT SIDE

This wall is located just east of Lake of the Domes. Park at the west end of Lamb Dome and hike up the gully between Mariuolumne and Medlicott Domes.

I   **The Cony** 5.8 (?, ?)
J   **Break Dancing** 5.9 (R, ?)
K   **Galadriel** 5.7 (?, ?)
L   **Return Engagement** 5.10 (?, ?)
M   **Sharky's End** 5.8 (PG/R)
N   **The Nazgul** 5.10b (PG)
O   **Testify** 5.12a (PG, ★)
P   **Black Rider** 5.10b (PG/R)
Q   **Sunstroke** 5.11a (?, ?)
DESCENT   Wander down 3rd and 4th class ledges on the eastern side of the dome.

LOST WALL

This 200 foot wall lies at the southern end of the Nazgul Wall (Mariuolumne Right Side). Follow the approach to that wall but continue right along its base, past a large, broad gully and on to the Lost Wall.

The Incredible Hulk 5.8   (?, ?) This route ascends the left side of **Lost Wall**, starting a short distance up the gully separating this wall and Mariuolumne Dome. The first pitch goes more or less straight up to a belay below a left slanting arch. Continue out left under the arch to its end, then work up and back right to a belay at a small pine. Work right, then up into a broken right facing corner that leads to the top.

MARIUOLUMNE DOME – Right Side

1 Break Dancing
2 Galadriel
3 Return Engagement
4 Sharky's End
5 The Nazgul
6 Black Rider

Working for Peanuts 5.10a (?, ?) Start just left of a conspicuous three-trunked tree. Climb up and left to a pin in an arch, then up and right to a bolt. Move up and left, then back right over a headwall. Easier climbing leads to a two-bolt belay not far from the top.

Runaway 5.9 (?, ?) A ledge runs along the right side of the wall, about twenty feet above the ground. Start near the left end of the ledge and climb over a tiny roof to a bolt. Continue up to a one-bolt belay just below the top.

Terrorist 5.10 (X, ?) Start just right of the preceeding route climbing over a roof and just right of a black streak. (free-solo)

Rock Vixen 5.7 (?, ?) Start 30 feet right of **Terrorist** and climb past a bolt in to right facing corners for one and a half pitches.

ISLAND IN THE SKY
1 Suicide Solution
2 Whip It
3 Prime Cut
4 Thunder Road
5 Freedom of Choice
6 Munge Plunge

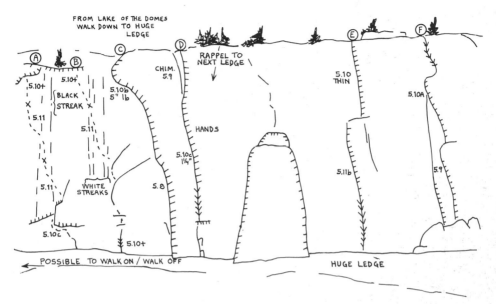

ISLAND IN THE SKY

This wall is found up high and left, on the north wall of Medlicott Dome. Park at the west end of Lamb Dome and hike up the gully between Mariuolumne Dome and Medlicott Dome. Then cut out right (west) on ledges and slabs to this 125 foot wall.

A **Suicide Solution** 5.11c (X, ★)
B **Whip It** 5.11b (X, ?)
C **Prime Cut** 5.10b (PG, ★)
D **Thunder Road** 5.10c (PG, ★ ★)
E **Freedom of Choice** 5.11b (PG, ★)
F **Munge Plunge** 5.10a (PG)

Chicken Little 5.9 (R, ★) Start 100 feet right of the **North Gully** in a short vertical crack. Continue up and left past five bolts to a two-pin belay. Climb a 5.7 pitch to a big ledge. Climb right slanting cracks for two 5.7 pitches then work up and left into the North Gully.

Pussey Paws 5.10 (R, ?) Start at **Chicken Little**, traverse right (5.10) then move up a thin crack past three bolts to a bolt belay. Climb up easy face to a roof, then climb past a bolt to a belay in a right slanting crack. Next, move up and left to the North Gully.

Another Country 5.7 (PG, ★) This can be seen as the left hand of two slanting cracks high on the north face of Medlicott. Approach this crack via low angle slabs to the left, or alternatively, by a more direct route up a deep and ominous chimney of the same crack system, left of North Gully. From the upper crack the climbing is stimulating, but somewhat dirty, for several pitches to the top.

MEDLICOTT DOME – Left Side

A Mariuolumne Dome
1 Hobbit Book
2 Super Chicken
3 Scorpion
4 Wailing Wall
5 The Yawn
6 Omega Race

7 Slipstream
8 West Face
9 The Middling
10 Friends in High Places
11 Slim Pickins
12 Sticks and Stones

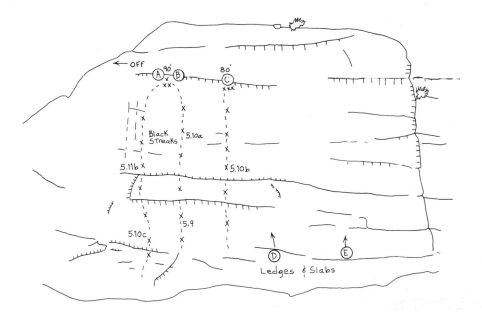

MEDLICOTT DOME — SOUTH FACE

Park at the west end of Lamb Dome and follow the right side of the gully that goes between Mariuolumne and Medlicott Domes. At the top and right is Lake of the Domes. This wall is above it on the backside of Medlicott Dome.

A **Damsel Fly** 5.11b (R, ?)
B **Yosemite Barking Toads** 5.10a (?, ?)
C **Right** 5.10b (?, ?)
D **South Face** 5.8 (?, ?)
E **Monster Walk** 5.8 (?, ?)

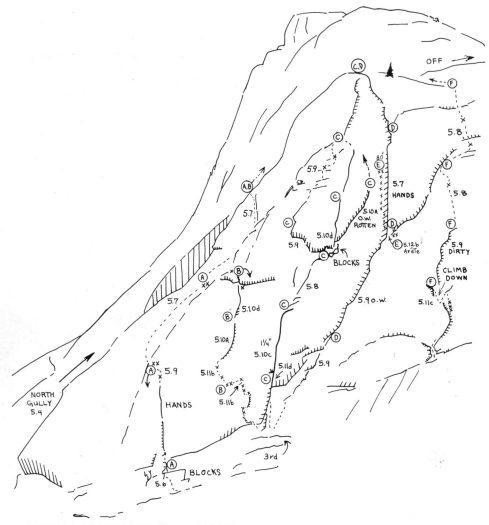

MEDLICOTT DOME — EAST
A **Super Chicken** 5.9 (R, ★)
B **Scorpion** 5.11b (PG, ★ ★)
C **Wailing Wall** 5.11d pro: small to 3 inch, esp. ¾ inch-1¼ inch (PG Center Route, ★ ★ ★)
D **The Yawn** 5.9 pro: to 4 inch (PG, ★ ★)
E **Lighter Side** 5.12b arête (PG, ★ ★ ★)
F **Black Magic** 5.11c (R/X)
DESCENT   Either hike down slabs at the western end of the dome or down the gully between Mariuolumne and Medlicott.

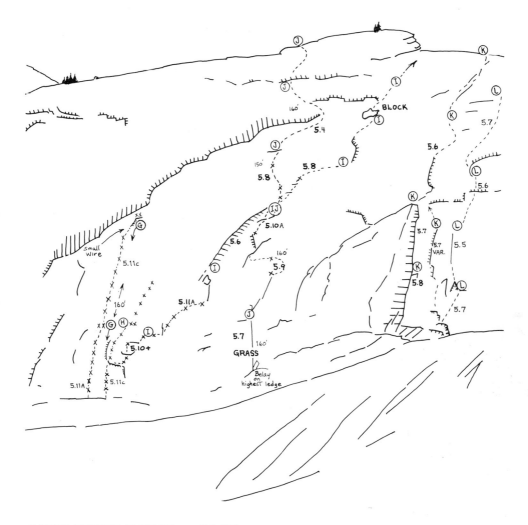

MEDLICOTT DOME — EAST
G   **Omega Race** 5.11c (PG/R, ★)
H   **Vapor Lock** 5.11c (PG, ★) unfinished
I   **Slipstream** 5.11c (PG/R, ★)
J   **Streamline** 5.10a (R)
K   **West Face** 5.8 (PG/R, ★)
L   **Fun House** 5.7 (R/X, ★)

MEDLICOTT DOME – Center

1 Friends in High Places
2 Sticks and Stones
3 Streamline
4 West Face
5 The Coming
6 White Line Fever
7 The Joystick
8 The Schneiderator
9 The SS
10 Two Cams Too Open

11 Ho Charlie
12 Royal Flush
13 Chartres
14 Spellbound
15 Shambles
16 Shipoopi!
17 Bachar-Yerian
18 Pretty in Pink Point
19 Raging Waters

MEDLICOTT DOME – Right

1 The Joystick
2 Ho Charlie
3 Royal Flush
4 Chartres
5 Shambles
6 Shipoopi!
7 Bachar-Yerian
8 Pretty in Pink Point
9 Raging Waters

10 Bogey Meets Mr. Porcupine
11 Swinger
12 You Asked For It
13 Sweet Jesus
14 Ciebola
15 Wrinkle in Time
16 The Kid
A West Farthing Dome

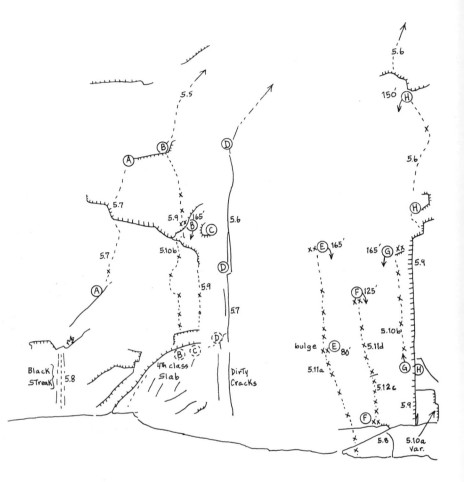

MEDLICOTT DOME — Middling/Coming Area

A **Bitter Creek** 5.8 (?, ?)
B **Bumps** 5.10b (PG, ★)
C **Blues in A** 5.9 (R, ★)
D **The Middling** 5.7 (?, ?)
E **Knuckle Ball** 5.11c (?, ?)
F **Show Don't Tell** 5.12c (?, ?)
G **Come and Get It** 5.10b (?, ?)
H **The Coming** 5.9 (PG, ★)

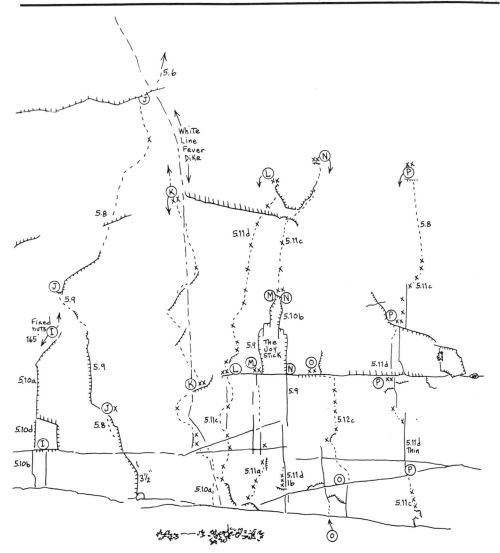

MEDLICOTT DOME – White Line Fever Area

I   **Second Coming** 5.10d (PG, ★)
J   **Breathing Hard** 5.9 (R, ★)
K   **White Line Fever** 5.11a (R)
L   **Dik Me A Dog** 5.11d (R)
M   **The Joystick** 5.11a (R/X)
N   **Pilot's License** 5.11d (RX, ?)
O   **The Schneiderato** 5.12c (R/X, ?)
P   **The SS** 5.11d (R/X, ?)

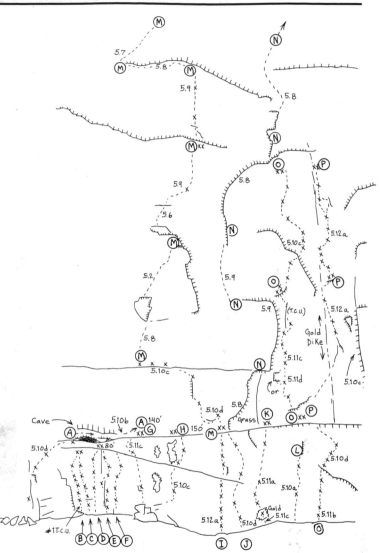

MEDLICOTT

A **Two Cams Too Open** 5.10d (R, ?)
B **Lone Ranger** 5.11d (PG, ★)
C **Material World** 5.11c (PG, ★)
D **Like A Virgin** 5.10c (R, ★)
E **Get Into The Groove** 5.11a (PG, ★)
F **Live To Tell** 5.11c (R)
G **Follow Your Heart** 5.11c (R/X)
H **Playing With A Full Deck** 5.10c (R/X)

I **Royal Flush** 5.12a (PG, ★★)
J **Space Rover** 5.10d (R/X)
K **Full House** 5.11c (?, ?)
L **Dazed and Confused** 5.11 (?, ?)
M **Hyper Space** 5.10d (R, ?)
N **Chartes** 5.9 (?, ?)
O **Priaprism** 5.11d (PG/R, ★)
P **Spellbound** 5.12a (?, ?)

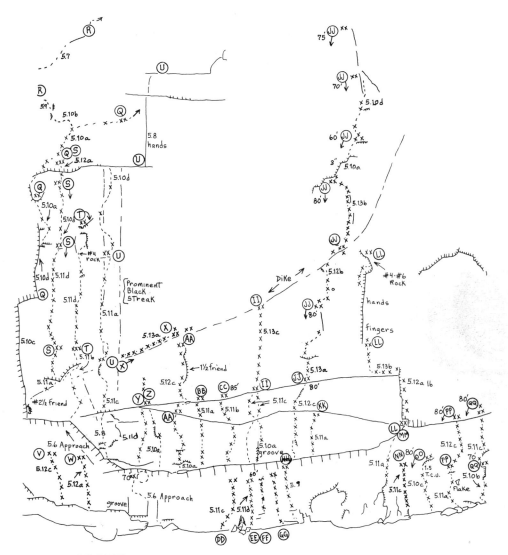

MEDLICOTT

Q **Shambles** 5.11b (R, ★)
R **Woodward Finish** 5.10b (?, ?)
S **Shipoopi!** 5.12a (PG/R, ★ ★ ★)
T **Slider-Banger** 5.11d (R, ★ ★)
U **Bachar/Yerian** 5.11c (X, ★ ★ ★)
V **Truth or Dare** 5.12c (PG, ★ ★)
W **Living in Sin** 5.12a (?, ?)
X **Bandaloop** 5.13a (PG, ★ ★ ★)
Y **Cat Spray** 5.11d (PG/R)
Z **Die Hard (Bachar Project)**
AA **Pretty in Pink Point** 5.12c (PG, ★)
BB **15 Seconds of Fame** 5.11a (PG, ★ ★)
CC **Big Time** 5.11b (PG, ★ ★)
DD **Dress Rehearsal** 5.11c (PG, ★)

EE **Lead Doll** 5.11d (PG, ★)
FF **King of the Hill** 5.12a (?, ?)
GG **Shady Rest** 5.10a (PG)
HH **Hill Crest Drive** 5.9 (?, ?)
II **Raging Waters** 5.13c (PG, ★)
JJ **Circus-Circus** 5.13b (PG, ★ ★)
KK **Shiner** 5.11a (PG, ★)
LL **Bogey Meets Mr. Porcupine** 5.13b
       (PG, ★)
MM **The Winery** 5.11a (R)
NN **Shell Shock** 5.11c (PG, ★)
OO **Drinking Buddies** 5.10c (R)
PP **Black Dahlia** 5.12c (?, ?)
QQ **Guy Takes A Bomma Gutsa** 5.11c (?, ?)

MEDLICOTT DOME— FAR WEST

Park at a spot just past the midpoint of the dome about 5.3 miles west of the Tuolumne Meadows Store. Walk around the west end of swamp and head toward the western end of Medlicott. An indistinct trail (the fishermans's trail to Cathedral Lakes) will be found that leads up through a blocky area to the base of an impressive orange wall. These routes lie on the right margin of that cliff.

A **Swinger** 5.11+ pro: many 1/8 inch-3/4 inch (R/X, ★)
B **You Asked For It** 5.10 pro: #3 Friend (X, ★ ★)
C **Sweet Jesus** 5.9+ (R)
D **One Toke Over the Line** 5.10c (R, ★)
E **Ciebola** 5.10b (PG, ★ ★ ★)
F **Swiss Orange Chip** 5.11c (R/X)
G **The Castoff** 5.11c (?, ?)
H **Ciebola Continuation** 5.10b (X, ?)
I **Alien** 5.11c (R, ★)
J **Wrinkle in Time** 5.11a (R, ★)
K **The Kid** 5.10b (X, ★)
L **The Pinhead** 5.11b (X, ★)
M **Here's Johnny** 5.10c (X, ★)
N **General Shortie** 5.10d (X, ★)

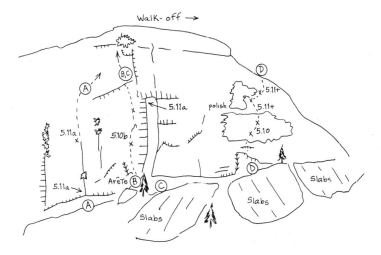

VIRGIN DOME

These routes are on a small dome just west of the Sticks and Stones dome.

A **Virgin Killer** 5.11a (R/X)
B **Ho Charlie** 5.10b (R/X)

C **No Bones** 5.11a (?, ?)
D **Virgin Testimony** 5.11+ (R)

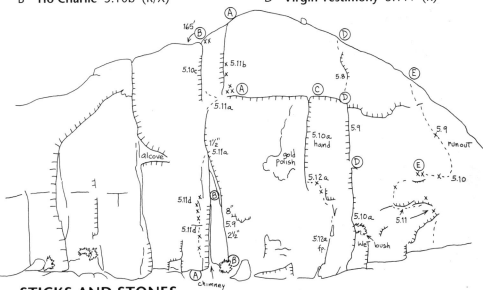

STICKS AND STONES

APPROACH This is the 200-foot dome located in front of the mid-section of Medlicott Dome below the climb, The Middling.

A **Centinella** 5.11d (R, ★)
B **Friends in High Places** 5.11a
C **Slim Pickins** 5.12a (R)
D **Sticks and Stones** 5.10a (PG, ★)
E **Lost in Face** 5.11 (R)

WEST FARTHING WALL
1 Two Bits Worth
2 Black Lite
3 Kryptonite
4 Master Samwise
5 Three Stooges
6 Sephyr

WEST FARTHING WALL

This wall is up and right (east) from the western end of Medlicott Dome. Approach by gaining an indistinct trail that leads up to and around the western end of Medlicott and on to Cathedral Lakes. From a point west of Medlicott, cross a stream to this rounded wall.

Pieces of Eight 5.8 (?, ?) Near the left end of the wall a right facing book is climbed nearly to its top. Continue up and left to the top of the wall.

Two Bits Worth 5.8 (?, ?) This route ascends a prominent dike which is perhaps 150 feet left of the center of the wall. The first pitch ends on a small ledge. Pitch two climbs past a bolt protected crux for one long rope length to the top.

Black Light 5.10b (R, ★) This route ascends a prominent black dihedral in the center of the wall. A bolt will be seen about 30 feet off the ground and below a roof. The first pitch climbs past this and ends at a two-bolt anchor. Next, climb a headwall past two bolts, then move up and left, then back right and on to the top.

Maniac's Maneuver 5.7 (?, ?) This starts in the middle of the wall. A right facing flake/corner leads to a bolt anchor. Climb over the ceiling about twenty feet right of the belay then on to the top.

Kryptonite 5.9 (?, ?) Start up **Maniac's Maneuver** then climb out right to a white flake and up past two bolts to a short crack. Continue up and right to a sling belay in a corner on a headwall. A zig-zag 5.8 pitch leads almost to the top.

Master Samwise 5.9 (R, ★) About 50 feet right of **Kryptonite**, climb up to a hole in the rock, then past a horizontal crack and two bolts to a belay below a roof. A 5.8 pitch leads almost to the top.

Three Stooges 5.8 (?, ?) Start about 50 feet right of **Master Samwise**, climb over a right-pointing flake and past two bolts to a vague corner. From its top, move right to a belay with a bolt and pin. Climb up, then left past a bolt and up to a roof. Above, easier climbing leads almost to the top.

Rock n' Rope 5.8 (R, ★) Start off a detached block 100 feet right of Three **Stooges**. Climb past several horizontal cracks and two bolts to a belay at a small roof. A pitch leads up and somewhat left, past a bolt and almost to the top.

Zephyr 5.7 This route is to the right of **Rock n' Rope** in a water streak just right of a lone tree on the face. Bridge across a gap at the base of the wall, then continue up an easy face, finally passing a bolt. Belay 30 feet higher. The second pitch avoids a headwall by traversing left before working back up and right to the top.

Save Our Soul 5.9 (?, ?) To reach this climb and **Cop Out**, walk all the way to the right side of the wall before moving back left on a ledge. This route starts from the lower left side of the ledge. Climb up and left past a bolt to a short left facing open book, then on to a large belay ledge. Continue up and left around a corner to the top.

Cop Out 5.8 (?, ?) This route starts in front of a group of trees about 100 feet right of the previous climb. Two bolts protect the first pitch that ends on the same ledge as **Save Our Soul**. Next, climb up and right under a headwall to the summit.

WEST FARTHING WALL/ DOZIER DOME

1	Black Light	4	Holdless Horror
2	Save Our Soul	5	Out of Gas
3	Cop Out	6	Ursula
A	Cathedral Peak	7	Tune Up
B	Eichorn Pinnacle	C	Well Hung Wall

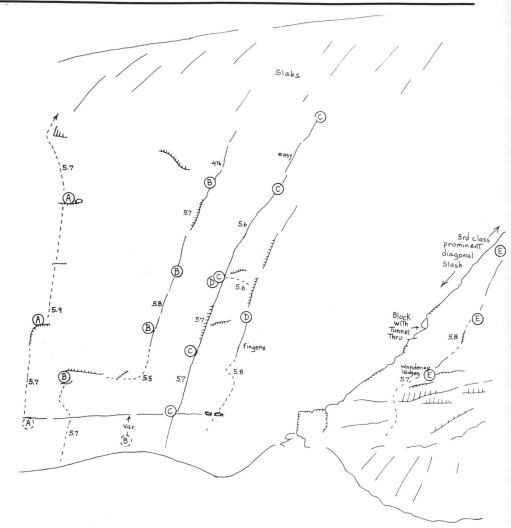

DOZIER DOME

This wall is between Medlicott Dome and Pywiack on the north side of the stream that drains Cathedral Lakes. Park one half mile east of Pywiack Dome and hike south for about one mile to the dome.

Easy Walk 5.6 (R, ?) At the left end of Dozier Dome, where the slabs come down into a very clean sandy area, are some straight-in crack systems that start about 50 feet off the ground. This route ascends the right crack for about three pitches.

Repo Man 5.9 (R/X) 100 feet right of **Easy Walk** is a group of large pine trees with some large horizontal crack/ledge systems above them. Start at the top of the second horizontal crack and climb about 40 feet to a bolt. Now climb out left onto easier rock and then back right to another bolt and then lead up to a ledge and belay. Easier climbing for two more pitches leads to the top.

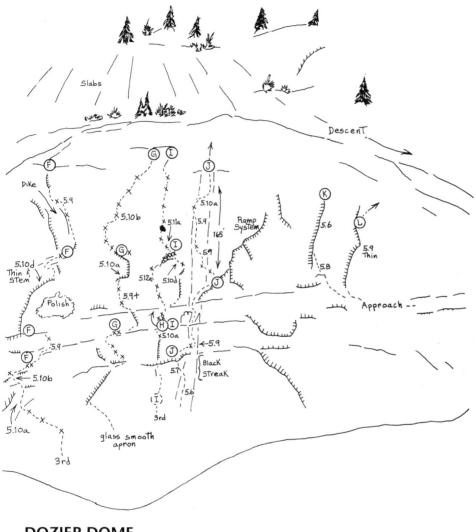

DOZIER DOME

A **Granite Garden** 5.9 (?, ?)
B **Stir Crazy** 5.8 (R/X)
C **Holdless Horror** 5.7 (PG, ★ ★)
D **Side Dish** 5.8 (PG)
E **Out of Bounds** 5.8 (PG)
F **Out of Gas** 5.10d (PG, ★)

G **Ursula** 5.10c (PG, ★ ★)
H **Claim Jumper** 5.12a (?, ?)
I **Angelic Upstart** 5.11a (PG/R, ★ ★)
J **Tune Up** 5.10a (?, ?)
K **After Thought** 5.8 (?)
L **Dozier Dihedral** 5.9 (PG)

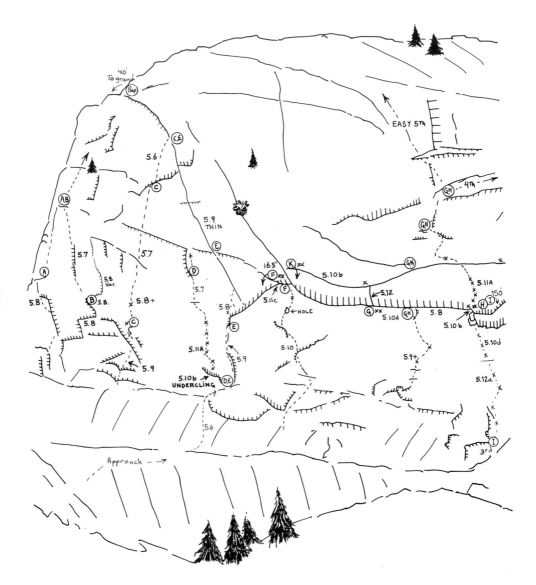

PYWIACK DOME

A **Pink Turds** 5.8 (R)
B **Up and Out** 5.8 (R)
C **Astroturf** 5.9 (R/X)
D **Unnatural Act** 5.11a (R/X)
E **Aqua Knobby** 5.9 (PG/R, ★ ★)
F **Pirouette Roof** 5.11c (R, ★)
G **Boa** 5.12 (R/X, ★)
H **Soft White Underbelly** 5.11a (R, ★ ★)
I **Heinous** 5.12a (?, ?)

DESCENT There are three possible descent routes from Pywiack Dome. A short rappel can be made down the east side, or the 5.4 route on the southwest slope can be down climbed. The routes of Boa through House Calls can be escaped by descending west on 3rd and 4th class slabs before the final headwall.

PYWIACK DOME

J   **Foott Route** 5.12a (R, ★)
K   **Forked Tongue** 5.10b (R, ★)
L   **Fort Knox** 5.11b (PG/R, ★ ★)
M   **Golden Bars** 5.11b (PG/R, ★ ★)

N   **Piece of Grass** 5.10d (X)
O   **Needle Spoon** 5.10a (PG, ★ ★ ★)
P   **Dike Route** 5.9 (R, ★ ★ ★)
Q   **House Calls** 5.6 (X, ★)

PYWIACK DOME

1. Astro Turf
2. Aqua Knobby
3. Pirouette Roof
4. Boa
5. Soft White Underbelly
6. Foott Route
7. Golden Bars
8. Piece of Grass
9. Needle Spoon
10. Dike Route
11. House Calls

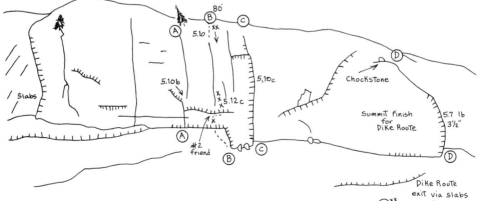

PYWIACK HEADWALL

These routes lie on the headwall above the **Foott Route**.

A **The Black Slot** 5.10b pro: stoppers & friends (?, ?)
B **Lover Not A Fighter** 5.12c pro: Big T.C.U.'s - set of friends (?, ?)
C **Who Stole My Flip-Flop** 5.10c (?, ?)
D **Dike Route** 5.9 (R, ★ ★ ★)

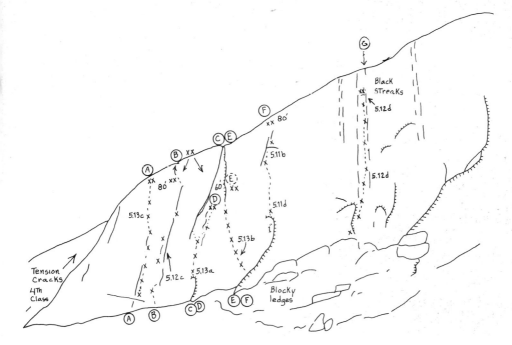

PYWIACK — SOUTHEAST FACE

Park at the western end of Pywiack Dome about 6.5 miles west of the Tuolumne Meadows Store. Follow the western slabs down low as they wind their way around to the eastern (backside) of Pywiack Dome.

A **Rising Sun** 5.13c (PG, ★ ★ ★)
B **Electric Africa** 5.12c pro: stoppers + T.C.U.'s (PG, ★ ★ ★)
C **Clash of the Titans** 5.13a pro: stoppers + T.C.U.'s (PG, ★ ★)
D **Medusa** 5.13a 1 bolt variation to **Clash of the Titans** (PG, ★)
E **European Vacatio**n 5.13b (PG, ★ ★)
F **The Meltdown** 5.11d pro: stoppers + T.C.U.'s (X, ★ ★)
G **Skin Walker** 5.12d (PG, ★ ★)

PENNYROYAL ARCHES

This cliff is best approached by skirting the west end of Pywiack Dome, a walk of about 20 minutes.

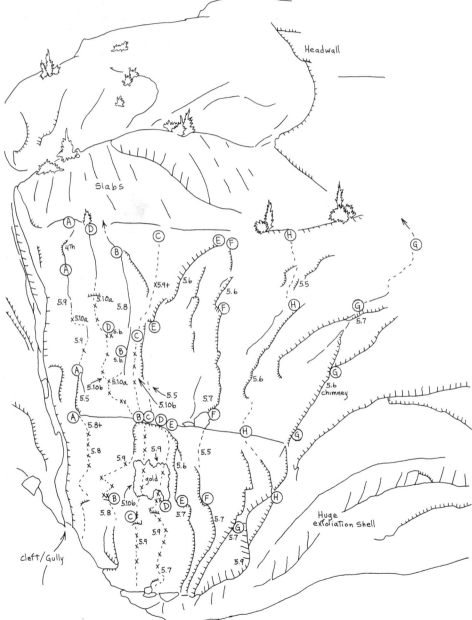

PENNYROYAL ARCHES
A **Ooze and Ahs** 5.10a (R, ★)
B **The Vision** 5.10a pro: tiny to 2 inch
(R, ★ ★)
C **Multiplication** 5.10b (R, ★ ★)
D **Alchemlsts' Re-vision** (R, ★ ★)
E **Eagle Dihedral** 5.7 (?, ?)
F **Euphoria** 5.7 (?, ?)

G **Pennyroyal High** 5.7 (?, ?)
H **The Hump** 5.9 (?, ?)
I **Walk About** 5.7 (?, ?)
J **U.F.R.** 5.10a (R, ★)
K **Diaphoretic Spasms** 5.9 (PG/R, ★)
L **White Slab** 5.7 (?, ?)
DESCEND down intricate 3rd class slabs to
the west or improbable ledges easl .

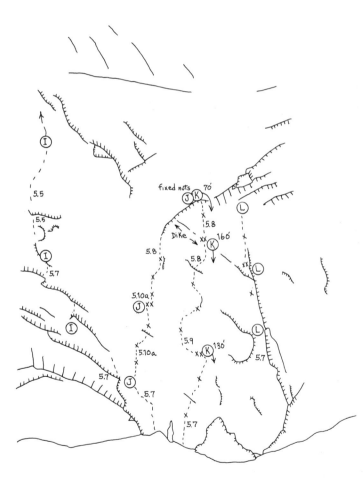

PENNYROYAL ARCHES

1 Ooze and Ahs
2 The Vision
3 Euphoria
4 Walk About

5 White Slab
6 Resisting Arrest
7 Whippersnapper

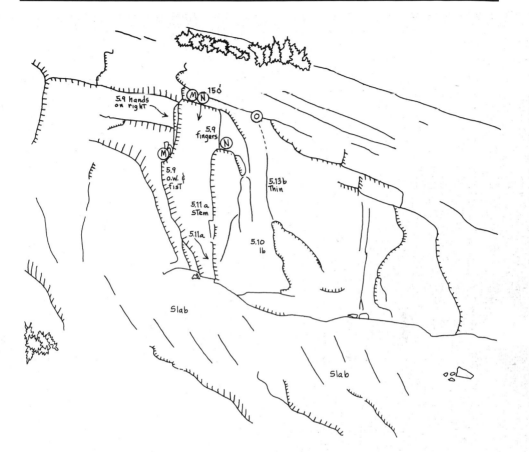

PENNYROYAL ARCHES HEADWALL

M **Disorderly Conduct** 5.9 (PG, ★)
N **Resisting Arrest** 5.11a pro: small to 2½ inch, esp ⅛ inch-1 ¼ inch (PG, ★ ★)
O **Whippersnapper** 5.13a (PG, ★ ★)

TENAYA PEAK
A   Tenaya Peak
B   Skyline Crags
C   The Power Wall
1   Tenaya Peak – Northwest Buttress
2   Barnacle Bill
3   Wimpy
4   Lakeshore Boulevard
5   Chimbote

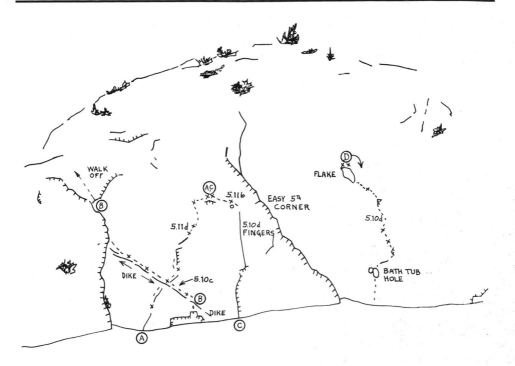

TENAYA PEAK WALL

This is the steeper wall that is just right of the toe of the Northwest Buttress. Approach from a parking lot at the east end of Tenaya Lake. Skirt the edge of the lake and hike up talus to the base of the wall.

A **Fierce Tiger on Rock** 5.11d (R)
B **Lakeshore Boulevard** 5.10c (R, ★)
C **Chimbote** 5.11b (R, ★)
D **Hole in One** 5.10d (?, ?)

Tenaya Peak — Northwest Butress (PG, ★ ★ ★) This long and striking buttress rises above Tenaya Lake and affords nebulous, though moderate, 5th class climbing to a spectacular summit and excellent view.

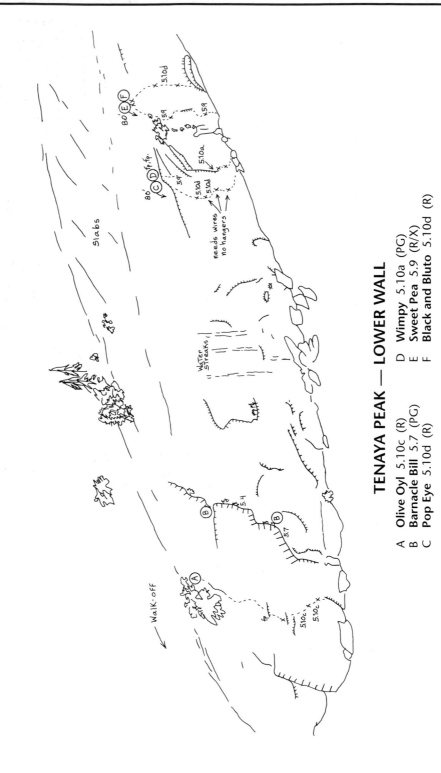

TENAYA PEAK — LOWER WALL

A Olive Oyl 5.10c (R)
B Barnacle Bill 5.7 (PG)
C Pop Eye 5.10d (R)

D Wimpy 5.10a (PG)
E Sweet Pea 5.9 (R/X)
F Black and Bluto 5.10d (R)

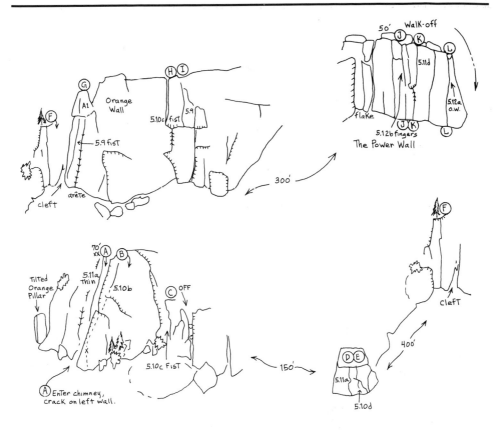

TENAYA PEAK — SKYLINE CRAGS & POWER WALL

These climbs are located up high on the western skyline of Tenaya Peak, where the cliffs meet talus at the far right side. The approach takes about 45 minutes.

A **Rapture of the Deep** 5.11a (PG, ★)
B **Sunset Prow** 5.10b (PG, ★)
C **Sharks Tooth** 5.10c (PG)
D **Liberal Apologist** 5.11a (PG)
E **Rabid Right** 5.10d (PG)
F **Buzzers and Hummers** 5.10c (?, ?)
G **Bar Gash** 5.9 A1 (PG)
H **Drunk n' Horney** 5.10c (PG, ?)
I **Mickey's Big Mouth** 5.9 (PG, ?)
J **Power of Soul** 5.12b (PG, ★ ★)
K **Soul Power** 5.11d (PG, ★ ★)
L **Quick Sand** 5.12a pro: many 3 inch-5 inch (PG, ★ ★)

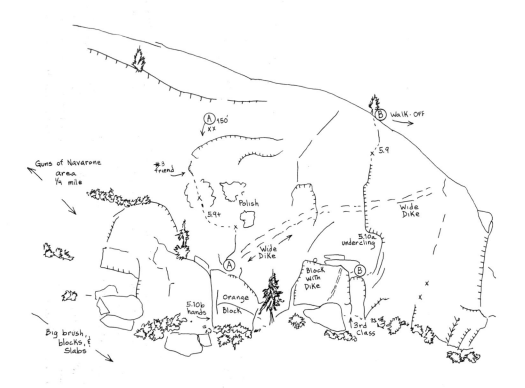

Guns of Navrone area ¼ mile

#3 friend

Ⓐ 150' XX

Polish

.9+

Ⓐ

5.10b hands

Orange Block

Wide Dike

Block with Dike

Ⓑ

3rd Class

Big brush, blocks, & Slabs

x 5.9

Wide Dike

5.10a undercling

Ⓑ WalK-off

GUNS OF NAVRONE & PROCTOLOGY WALL

Several fun short top ropes are found at the Guns of Navrone Area. About 9.3 miles west of the Tuolumne Meadows Store or .6 miles back east from Olmstead Point, park in a paved turnout almost at the bottom of the big hill. The Wall is hidden in trees across the way just below a small dome. Hike down across the meadow and up the slabs on the other side. The Proctology Wall is the western side of the small dome that forms the summit of the ridge.

A   **Frontier Proctologist** 5.10b (?, ?)
B   **Pigmy Pony** 5.10a pro: to 3½ inch (?, ?)

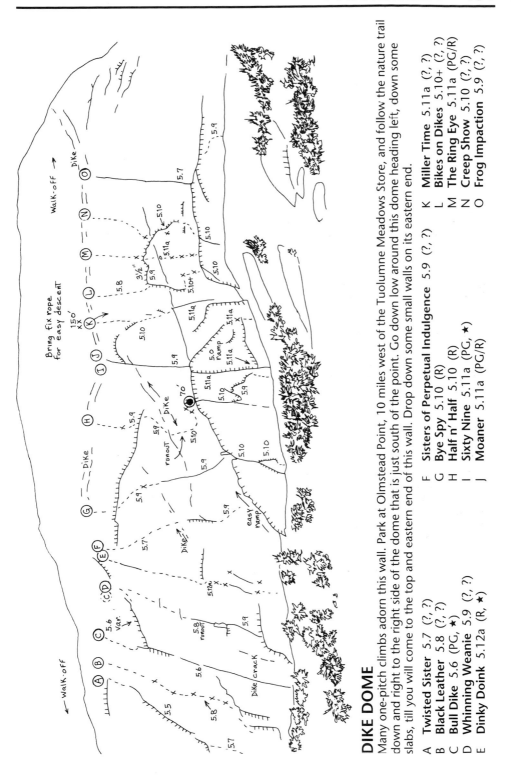

DIKE DOME

Many one-pitch climbs adorn this wall. Park at Olmstead Point, 10 miles west of the Tuolumne Meadows Store, and follow the nature trail down and right to the right side of the dome that is just south of the point. Go down low around this dome heading left, down some slabs, till you will come to the top and eastern end of this wall. Drop down some small walls on its eastern end.

A Twisted Sister 5.7 (?, ?)
B Black Leather 5.8 (?, ?)
C Bull Dike 5.6 (PG, ★)
D Whinning Weanie 5.9 (?, ?)
E Dinky Doink 5.12a (R, ★)

F Sisters of Perpetual Indulgence 5.9 (?, ?)
G Bye Spy 5.10 (R)
H Half n' Half 5.10 (R)
I Sixty Nine 5.11a (PG, ★)
J Moaner 5.11a (PG/R)

K Miller Time 5.11a (?, ?)
L Bikes on Dikes 5.10+ (?, ?)
M The Ring Eye 5.11a (PG/R)
N Creep Show 5.10 (?, ?)
O Frog Impaction 5.9 (?, ?)

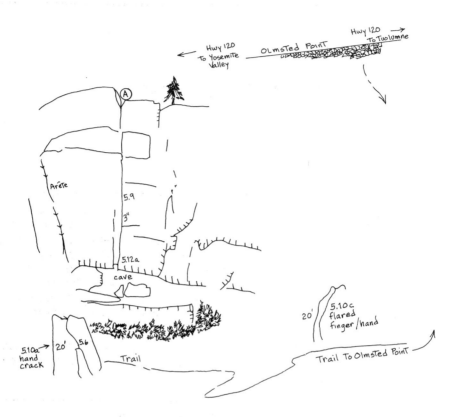

OLMSTEAD POINT

APPROACH From the center of the large parking area at Olmstead Point, gain a trail that cuts back right below the parking lot. Hike back right on the trail to this 40-foot cliff.

Lord of the Apes 5.12a pro: to 3 1/2 inch (PG, ★)

SPORT CLIMBS

HERE IS A LIST OF CLIMBS THAT are semi- to well-protected, requiring a minimum of gear. Tuolumne has always had a reputation for scary runout climbs, but in recent years, many excellent sport routes have been put up. They usually will have 3⁄8-inch bolts with the shorter climbs (80 feet or less) set up for easy lower-offs. Unfortunately, you will probably notice that the majority are 5.11 and harder. All the easier terrain was taken up in earlier years by good climbers or by free soloers. Some of the great new areas include Central Medlicott, with its beautiful, vertical, orange-knobbed wall; East Cottage Dome with its killer 5.10 steep face routes, and the Tioga Pass area, which offers overhanging climbs on excellent rock unlike that of Tuolumne.

When needed a pro list will be included but you should probably bring a small rack to the base just in case. 80 feet refers to one doubled rope, 165 feet refers to two (2) 165 feet ropes needed to rappel off the climb.

5.6

Hot Crossed Buns ★ low angle slab, bolts, 165 feet. Page 37.

5.7

The Golfers Route ★★★ 6 bolts, knobs, 2 pitches, bring rack of small wireds and tcu's for pro and the belay at the top of the first, TCU's needed on 2nd pitch. 5 bolts; 165 feet. Page 44.

Mere Image ★ low angle slab that follows a polished dike, a little runout, bolts; 165 feet. Page 39.

Wild in the Streaks ★ low angle slab, little run, bolts; 165 feet. Page 37.

5.8

Biscuit and Gravy ★ low angle slab, bolts, friends #1 to 2.5; 165 feet. Page 37.

5.9

Hill Crest Drive ★★ 80 feet. Page 129.

5.10a

Needle Spoon ★★★ knobs, thin face, 6 bolts 1st pitch, rappel 165 feet or do semi runout 2nd. Page 139.

Shady Rest ★ knobs and edges; 80 feet. Page 129.

Darth Vader's Revenge ★★★ 10a vertical to overhanging knobs. 8 bolts on first, 3 bolts on 2nd; 165 feet. Page 44.

Pretty in Pink Point ★★ first pitch, vertical knobs, crux is going past small roof, bolts; 80 feet. Page 129.

5.10b

Ciebola ★★★   thin face and knobs wireds for 1st, many bolts on 2nd; 165 feet. Page 130.

Fuel Rod ★   steep climbing on some good edges, bolts; 80 feet. Page 39.

5.10c

Knobulator ★   knobs bolts; 80 feet. Page 62.

Prognosis ★   steep knobs and edges, bolts; 80 feet. Page 61.

Shadow of Doubt ★★★   steep knobs bolts, rappel; 165 feet. Page 48.

Spark Plug ★   steep face, bolts; 50 feet. Page 71.

5.10d

Rover Take Over ★★   steep knobs and edges, bolts; 80 feet. Page 62.

Knobnoxious ★★★   steep knobs and edges, bolts; 80 feet. Page 62.

Table of Contents ★★   thin face bolts, rappel 165 feet after 2nd or do semi runout 3rd. Page 23.

Knobvious ★★★   steep knobs, bolts, little runout at top; 80 feet. Page 62.

Platapus ★   steep knobs to overhang, wireds, little run to 1st bolt; 80 feet. Page 61.

5.11a

Get into the Groove ★   knobs and lie backing up a steep groove, little run; 80 feet. Page 128

The Ledge ★   steep face, 3 bolts; 80 feet. Page 21.

Orange Plasma ★★★   steep knobs, wireds, little run to 1st bolt; 80 feet. Page 62.

15 Seconds of Fame ★★   great steep knob climb off of the awesome Bachar-Yerian ledge; 85 feet. Page 129.

5.11b

Walk Like An Egyptian ★   vertical face on the **Transpire Wall;** bolts, 2.5 friend; 80 feet. Page 77.

Rat Patrol   steep edges and small arete; 80 feet. Page 77.

Big Time ★★   steep knobs and edges, bolts; 165 feet. Page 129.

Torqued ★★★   steep cutter edges, bolts; 80 feet. Page 82.

5.11c

Dress Rehearsal ★   thin edges and slopers; 80 feet. Page 129.

Ground Effects ★★   steep knobs and edges to a heinous thin slab; 80 feet. Page 110.

Paiste Formula ★★   thin face, bolts, rappel top of 1st; 165 feet. Page 34.

Midnight Hour ★★   .5+1 tcu, 3 bolts, steep face, horizontals; 80 feet. Page 53.

Jiffy Pop ★★   vertical knobs and edges; 70 feet. Page 69.

Le Papillon ★★   vertical to overhanging knobs; 70 feet. Page 69.

Executive Decision ★   small wireds, tcu's, bolts on steep face and horizontals, little run; 80 feet. Page 80.

Roadkill ★★   bolted steep face, edges; 60 feet. Page 42.

5.11d

Shipoopi! ★★★ even though rated 5.12a, the first and second pitch are 11d with the second pitch being the all time calf pumper on steep knobs, little run to first bolt, 3 friend some tcu's, one medium wired, rappel; 165 feet. Page 129.

Bag O' Tricks ★★ watch out for the moves through a roof, .5-1.5 tcus's; 80 feet. Page 83.

Poindexter ★★ fun little climb through some roofs; 60 feet. Page 83.

Public Enemy ★★ 4 bolts on vertical knobs and weird mantle; 80 feet. Page 39.

Scratch N's Sniff ★★★ killer combination moves up a vertical and overhanging wall, 3/4 and 2 friend; 80 feet. Page 77.

Itchy Scratchy ★★★ killer combination moves up a steep and overhanging wall, 2.5 friend for start; 80 feet. Page 77.

Diagnosis ★★ steep knobs and face, bolts; 80 feet. Page 61.

Trickanosis ★★ steep knobs and edges, bolts; 80 feet. Page 61.

Lone Ranger ★★ overhanging and vertical knobs, bolts, .5-1 inch for start; 165 feet. Page 128.

Cat Spray ★ hard first moves, steep knobs, bolts; 165 feet. Page 129.

5.12a

Wicked Shortie ★★ short but hard, 30 second approach; 40 feet. Page 84.

EZ Does It ★★★ good warm up moves on overhanging wall to a poor dyno, beautiful setting; 80 feet. Page 85.

Go With The Flow ★ tricky climbing up a groove, bolts ¾ to 1½ feet pro, 80 feet. Page 65.

Osmosis ★ steep small knobs and edges; 70 feet. Page 61.

Neurosis ★★ sloper knobs, bolts; 70 feet. Page 61.

Quantum Leap ★ vertical edges, bolts; 80 feet. Page 65.

Wild Streak ★★ vertical overhanging knobs, wireds tcu's, bolts; 80 feet. Page 48.

Angel Eyes ★ steep slab face, 5 bolts; 80 feet. Page 44.

Cupcake ★★★ vertical and overhanging knobs, bolts; 80 feet. Page 68.

Straightaway ★ steep knobs, bolts, 4 bolts; 80 feet. Page 71.

Blue Moon ★ steep knobs, 5 bolts; 80 feet. Page 71.

Royal Flush ★★ steep slab face with knobs, bolts 2 rope rappel. Page 128.

Spell Bound ★ thin face, thin to medium pro, rappel 2 ropes. Page 128.

Spiro Gyro ★ rounded vertical groove; 50 feet, 5 bolts. Page 65.

Wicked Itchy ★★★ follow a series of arete's to the final wicked overhanging lieback, bolts but hard clips for short people down low; 165 feet. Page 77.

The Ugly Arête ★★ vertical arete, 5 bolts; 80 feet. Page 42.

Bodycount ★★ vertical and overhanging knobs and edges, 13 bolts; 165 feet. Page 45.

5.12b

We Want EZ ★★★ Overhanging edges to thin crack to a wild arete finish; 80 feet. Page 85.

Silver Bullet ★★★ a most killer double overhanging corner with the crux at the top, bolts; 165 feet. Page 83.

Felix ★★ outrageous moves through roofs to a vertical wall, bolts; 80 feet. Page 83.

Master Cylinder ★★★ wild moves up an overhanging shallow corner with the crux a hard step right; 80 feet. Page 81.

Quick Release ★★ overhanging edges, 4 bolts; 40 feet. Page 42.

Red Don't Go ★★ moves up an overhanging wall then through a roof, 3 friend; 50 feet. Page 77.

Heat Sensitive ★ vertical knobs thin face, 6 bolts, stick clip 1st bolt; 80 feet. Page 29.

Iya ★★ vertical overhanging cutter edges, bring 1 through 2.5 friend for start then bolt pro, two rope technique for start to 1st bolt; 80 feet. Page 82.

Realativity ★ vertical edges, lieback, bolts; 80 feet. Page 65.

Rebel Yell ★★ vertical overhanging knobs cutter edges, bolts; 80 feet. Page 53.

Dough Boy ★ hard moves between horizontal cracks, 2 bolts; 80 feet. Page 68.

Icing ★★★ vertical knobs, well worth the hike, bolts; 80 feet. Page 68.

Wicked Stiffy ★★ overhanging face, 3 bolts; 40 feet. Page 77.

Shut It Up ★ vertical face, bolts.

The Lighter Side ★★★★ overhanging arete, climb 2 pitches of yawn, arete out left. Bolts, bring pro for yawn, best pitch on Midlicott; 165 feet. Page 122.

5.12c

Truth or Dare ★★ vertical and overhanging knobs; 80 feet. Page 129.

Spike ★ combo climbing up vertical to overhanging wall; 80 feet. Page 82.

The Finger ★★ steep edge and combo climbing, little run; 165 feet. Page 83.

Pretty in Pink Point ★★★ vertical knobs and lieback, bolts; 165 feet. Page 129.

Patticake ★★ vertical knobs with very thin edge crux, bolts; 80 feet. Page 68.

Synchronicity ★ vertical edges, lieback, bolts; 80 feet. Page 65.

Shadow Warriors ★★★ steep face-knobs, bolts; 80 feet. Page 45.

Black Dahlia ★★ steep slab, 2 pitches, 1st pitch a little runout, can get off with one rope. Page 129.

5.12d

Rap It Up ★★★ overhanging face knobs, bolts; 80 feet. Page 48.

Fame and Fortune ★★ vertical overhanging face knobs, bolts; 80 feet. Page 45.

Mystery Achievement steep thin face to easier knobs, bolts; 165 feet. Page 48.

Laser Blade ★★★★ overhanging arete, 6 bolts; 80 feet. Page 42.

Cruise Control ★★★ vertical and overhanging knobs, 7 bolts; 80 feet. Page 110

Ice ★★ vertical face, 7 bolts; 80 feet. Page 112.

Perhaps, Another Bowl? ★★★ small hands to a killer stepped overhang then blanks out at the lip, #2 + 2½ friend forstart; 40 feet. Page 69.

Skin Walker ★★ knobs and intricate combo moves up a overhanging groove crack; 80 feet. Page 141.

5.13a

Medusa ★ one bolt variation to Clash of the Titans, if you want to avoid the crack on the last part of Clash to this way; 70 feet. Page 141.

Bandaloop ★★★ very slippery traverse on a outrageous orange dike; 165 feet. Page 129.

The Grapevine ★★★ killer overhanging edges, 6 bolts; 80 feet. Page 65.

Helter Skelter very, very thin edging on an 85-degree wall. Page 24.

Sudden Impact ★ vertical face, 6 bolts; 80 feet. Page 65.

Clash of the Titans ★★ vertical knobs, 3 bolts, 2+3 friend; 80 feet. Page 141.

5.13b

Bogey Meets Mr. Procupine ★★ lieback to thin face traverse, 8 bolts rappel after 1st; 165 feet. Page 129.

European Vacation ★★★ vertical knobs, 5 bolts; 80 feet. Page 141.

Love Sexy ★★ vertical knobs-edges, 8 bolts; 80 feet (smashed hangers). Page 45.

Super Sonic ★★ vertical knobs-edges, 6 bolts, 2 friend; 80 feet. Page 45.

Circus-Circus ★★ one of the longest, most sustained climbs in the Meadows. Thin edges and liebacking up a groove; 165 feet. Page 129.

5.13c

Raging Waters ★★★ vertical to overhanging knobs, many bolts; 165 feet. Page129.

Rising Sun ★★★ thin edges on an overhanging wall, very photogenic; 70 feet. Page 141.

ROUTES BY RATING

5.8

- ☐ Acme Crack (PG) 12
- ☐ After Thought   137
- ☐ Alimony Cracks (PG) ★ 58
- ☐ Apparition (R) ★ 57
- ☐ Back to the Bar   15
- ☐ Back to the Future (X) 75
- ☐ Big Business (PG) 69
- ☐ Birthday Party   108
- ☐ Biscuit and Gravy (PG) ★ 37
- ☐ Bitter Creek   126
- ☐ Black Leather   151
- ☐ Black Sheep   108
- ☐ Block, The Right (R) 39
- ☐ Blue Moon (X) 107
- ☐ Buckets of Blood   12
- ☐ Charge Card (PG) 69
- ☐ Cony, The   116
- ☐ Cop Out   133
- ☐ Delta Squeeze   36
- ☐ Dog Dome—North Face   76
- ☐ East Cottage Regular Route (R) 62
- ☐ El Condor (R/X) ★★ 57
- ☐ Elephant's Massacre (R) ★ 75
- ☐ Face to Face (R) 48
- ☐ Grease Monkey (PG) 18
- ☐ Great Pumpkin (PG/R) ★★ 105
- ☐ Hit Or Miss (R) 37
- ☐ Holiday on Rock (PG/R) ★ 91
- ☐ Honeymoon's Over (PG) ★ 58
- ☐ Human Fly Trap (X) 75
- ☐ Incredible Hulk, The   116
- ☐ Ivory Tower Left (PG) ★ 18
- ☐ Juvenile Delinquent (R) 91
- ☐ Left Crack (PG/R) 109

- ☐ Levy's Lament (PG) 36
- ☐ Lotsa Balls (R/X) 44
- ☐ Magical Mystery Tour (R) ★★★ 107
- ☐ Middle of the Road (X) 75
- ☐ Minotaur (PG/R) ★ 87
- ☐ Monster Walk   121
- ☐ Motzah Balls (R/X) 44
- ☐ Pieces of Eight   133
- ☐ Pink Turds (R) 138
- ☐ Prime Time (R) ★ 48
- ☐ R.C.A. (R) ★ 57
- ☐ Right Water Crack (R) ★ 74
- ☐ Rivendell Crack (PG) 45
- ☐ Rock n' Rope (R) ★ 133
- ☐ Seconds to Darkness (PG) ★ 113
- ☐ Sharky's End (PG/R) 116
- ☐ Shrouds Have No Pockets (PG) ★ 115
- ☐ Side Dish (PG) 137
- ☐ Snooze You Lose   71
- ☐ Sorry Dave   71
- ☐ South Crack (R) ★★★ 24
- ☐ Stir Crazy (R/X) 137
- ☐ Strider (PG) 115
- ☐ Sunny Delight   36
- ☐ Tapwork Orange (PG/R) ★ 75
- ☐ Three Stooges   133
- ☐ Two Bits Worth   133
- ☐ Ugly Face   68
- ☐ Up and Out (R) 138
- ☐ Walk in the Park, A   68
- ☐ Werner's Wiggle (R) ★★ 74
- ☐ West Face (PG/R) ★ 123
- ☐ Who's The Bosch ★ 52

5.9

- ☐ Ages Apart (R) 44
- ☐ Aqua Knobby (PG/R) ★★ 138
- ☐ Astroturf (X) 138
- ☐ Babe Roof (PG/R) 25
- ☐ Bachar Solo (X) 44
- ☐ Bar Gash 5.9; A1 (PG) 149
- ☐ Battlescar Galactipus (PG) 12
- ☐ Becky's Corner   71
- ☐ Belay o' Matic (R) 48
- ☐ Big Dog Hammer (PG/R) ★ 75
- ☐ Billiard Room (PG) ★ 65
- ☐ Black Diamond (X) 37
- ☐ Black Widow (R) ★ 44
- ☐ Block, Left Side (PG) 39
- ☐ Blues in A (R) ★ 126
- ☐ Boat Party (PG) 49

- ☐ Borderline   58
- ☐ Botch (R) 25
- ☐ Brainwave (R/X) 52
- ☐ Break Dancing (R) 116
- ☐ Breathing Hard (R) ★ 127
- ☐ Camel Walk (PG/R) 25
- ☐ Chartes   128
- ☐ Chicken Little (R) ★ 119
- ☐ Childhood's End (PG/R) ★ 48
- ☐ Coming, The (PG) ★ 126
- ☐ Cooler, The (PG/R) ★ 41
- ☐ Cry in Time Again (PG) ★★★ 73
- ☐ Cuckoo's Nest (R) 46
- ☐ Curve Like Her (R) ★ 31
- ☐ Dead Next Door (PG) 21
- ☐ Deadheads Delight (R) 54

5.9

- [ ] Deimos (PG) ★★★ 41
- [ ] Desert Highway (PG) 13
- [ ] Diaphoretic Spasms (PG/R) ★ 143
- [ ] Dike Route (R) ★★★ 139
- [ ] Discount Crack 70
- [ ] Disorderly Conduct (PG) ★ 145
- [ ] Dixie Peach (PG) ★ 24
- [ ] Dozier Dihedral (PG) 137
- [ ] Drafted (R) 39
- [ ] Duoich Mark 18
- [ ] Fairview Regular Route (PG) ★★★ 97
- [ ] Family Affair (PG/R) 44
- [ ] Faux Pas (PG) ★ 34
- [ ] Fist Fight 60
- [ ] Frog Impaction 151
- [ ] G-Spot (PG) ★ 75
- [ ] Gold Mind (G) ★ 85
- [ ] Gortlough RA 20
- [ ] Grantie Garden 137
- [ ] Green Eggs and Ham (PG/R) 54
- [ ] Green Goblin (R) ★ 108
- [ ] Grey Ghost (R/X) 57
- [ ] Higgy Stardust 110
- [ ] Hill Crest Drive 129
- [ ] Hired Drill (PG/R) ★ 75
- [ ] Hump, The 143
- [ ] Integration (R) ★★ 75
- [ ] Joe Mamba (PG/R) ★ 36
- [ ] Kick Back Crack (PG) 65
- [ ] King Midas (R) ★ 106
- [ ] Kryptonite 133
- [ ] Lampoon 110
- [ ] Late for Dinner Again (R) 64
- [ ] Lembert Dome—Northwest Buttress (PG/R) 73
- [ ] Lieback Detector 36
- [ ] Lips (X) 75
- [ ] Litho Lux (R) ★ 48
- [ ] Luke Skywalker (R) 44
- [ ] Lunar Leap (R) ★ 74
- [ ] Master Samwise (R) ★ 133
- [ ] Medlicott Dome—South Face 121
- [ ] Mickey's Big Mouth (PG) 149
- [ ] Mop and Glow (PG) 91
- [ ] My Dove Bear (X) 21
- [ ] Namche Bazaar (R) 34
- [ ] Nerve Wrack Point (R) 110
- [ ] Offday (R) 91
- [ ] On the Lamb (PG) ★★ 110
- [ ] Out of Bounds (PG) 137
- [ ] Overexposure (X) 75
- [ ] Passover (R) 108
- [ ] Pebble Beach (PG/R) 52
- [ ] Phobos (PG) ★★★ 41
- [ ] Pippin (PG/R) ★ 34
- [ ] Pleasant View Arête 12
- [ ] Powell Route (PG) 97
- [ ] Pumpkin Eater (R) 107
- [ ] Quaking Aspen (PG) ★★ 80
- [ ] Quiet Desperation (R) ★ 24
- [ ] Rad School (X) ★ 75
- [ ] Repo Man (R/X) 136
- [ ] Right Crack (PG/R) 109
- [ ] Roadkill (R) ★★ 13
- [ ] Roadrunner (PG) ★ 13
- [ ] Rocky Horror (R) ★ 75
- [ ] Roseanne (R) ★★ 105
- [ ] Runaway 117
- [ ] Save Our Soul 133
- [ ] Shoot the Moon (R/X) 74
- [ ] Sisters of Perpetual Indulgence 151
- [ ] Sleeper (R) 110
- [ ] Solitary Confinement ★★★ 107
- [ ] Stalag 13 83
- [ ] Stick and Span (PG) ★ 50
- [ ] Streakin' (PG) 75
- [ ] Super Chicken (R) ★ 122
- [ ] Sweet Pea (R/X) 148
- [ ] T.H. Sea (PG/R) 57
- [ ] Take A Whizz (PG) 46
- [ ] Tales from the Crypt (R) 57
- [ ] Thin Air (R) 34
- [ ] Time Warp (R/X) 75
- [ ] Tittely Winks (R) ★ 53
- [ ] Too Pooped To Pop (PG) ★ 48
- [ ] Trick Shot (PG) ★ 65
- [ ] Truck n' Drive (R) ★★ 74
- [ ] Two Left Shoes (R) 64
- [ ] Walk of Life (X) 107
- [ ] Wanderer, The 68
- [ ] West Crack (PG) ★★★ 56
- [ ] Whinning Weanie 151
- [ ] Whore That Ate Chicago, The 29
- [ ] Witch o' The West (PG/R) 56
- [ ] Yawn, The (PG) ★★ 122
- [ ] Zulu Lulu (PG) 49

5.9+

- ☐ Booty and the Beach (R) 73
- ☐ Crescent Arch (PG) ★★★ 57
- ☐ Gold Wall 81
- ☐ Hobbitation (R) 41
- ☐ Moon Dawg 86
- ☐ Stomper (PG) ★ 115
- ☐ Sweet Jesus (R) 130
- ☐ Talk Dirty To Me (PG) 18

5.10a

- ☐ Ace in the Hole (R/X) 54
- ☐ Achilles Last Stand (R) ★ 32
- ☐ Astrovan (R) 32
- ☐ Carpet Crawler (R) 110
- ☐ Chariots of the Todds (R) 51
- ☐ Climbing Club (R) ★ 24
- ☐ Continuation (R) 110
- ☐ Cooke Book (PG) ★★ 56
- ☐ Cottage Cheese (PG) ★ 60
- ☐ Darth Vader's Revenge (PG) ★★★ 44
- ☐ Deception (PG/R) ★ 46
- ☐ Don't Exchange Bodily Fluids (R) 39
- ☐ Dos Equis (PG/R) ★ 75
- ☐ Dukey Corner (R) 110
- ☐ Fairies Wear Boots (R) ★ 32
- ☐ Falk's Folly (R) 82
- ☐ Fiddler on the Roof (R) 97
- ☐ Fingertips (PG/R) ★★ 58
- ☐ Flipper (R) 31
- ☐ Fool's Gold (PG/R) ★ 57
- ☐ Freakin' (R/X) 75
- ☐ Go Cat Go (TR) 70
- ☐ Great Circle (PG) ★★ 58
- ☐ Great White Arête (X) 23
- ☐ Harlot (R) 29
- ☐ Head Cheese (R) 60
- ☐ Head Rush (R/X) ★ 74
- ☐ Hoodwink (PG) ★★ 29
- ☐ Invader (PG) ★ 82
- ☐ Ivory Tower Center (PG) ★ 18
- ☐ Jungle Book 41
- ☐ Lament (R/X) 110
- ☐ Latin Lady (R/X) ★ 44
- ☐ Little Sheba (PG) 110
- ☐ March of Dimes (PG/R) 54
- ☐ Mega Bleam 73
- ☐ Middle Earth (PG) ★★ 115
- ☐ Miss Apprehension (PG) 18
- ☐ Missile Toe (PG) 18
- ☐ Moose and Squirrel 86
- ☐ Motivated by Food (R) ★ 73
- ☐ Munge Plunge (PG) 119
- ☐ Needle Spoon (PG) ★★★ 139
- ☐ New Tricks for Old Dogs (R) 54
- ☐ Not Quite Right (PG/R) 48
- ☐ One for the Money 70
- ☐ One Size Fits All 69
- ☐ Ooze and Ahs (R) ★ 143
- ☐ Pebbles and Bam Bam (R) 59
- ☐ Pencil-Necked Geek (PG) ★ 60
- ☐ Peter, Peter (R) ★ 106
- ☐ Pigmy Poney 150
- ☐ Pokin' the Pup (R) 32
- ☐ Pop Fly 71
- ☐ Rawl Drive (R/X) 74
- ☐ Shady Rest (PG) 129
- ☐ Short Change (PG) ★ 18
- ☐ Shy Tuna (PG/R) 25
- ☐ Smiling at Wilee (PG) ★★ 13
- ☐ Snap Crackle and Pop (R/X) 75
- ☐ Sticks and Stones (PG) ★ 131
- ☐ Straight Street (R/X) ★★ 107
- ☐ Streamline (R) 123
- ☐ Summertime (R/X) 50
- ☐ Tom Tom 43
- ☐ Touch of Grey (R) 54
- ☐ Transpire Crack (PG) 77
- ☐ Tricks Are For Kids (X) 75
- ☐ Tune Up 137
- ☐ Tweekin' (R/X) ★ 75
- ☐ U.F.R. (R) ★ 143
- ☐ Undisputed Truth (PG/R) 34
- ☐ Unh-Huh (R) ★ 105
- ☐ Urban Perversion (R) 51
- ☐ Vision, The (R) ★★ 143
- ☐ Way We Were, The (PG/R) 24
- ☐ Wimpy (PG) 148
- ☐ Working for Peanuts 117
- ☐ Yosemite Barking Toads 121
- ☐ You Asked For It (X) ★★ 130
- ☐ Your Soft Sundae (X) 21

5.10b

- [ ] American Wet Dike   34
- [ ] American Wet Dream (PG) ★★ 34
- [ ] Ballroom Dancing (R/X) 62
- [ ] Black Bart (R) ★ 56
- [ ] Black Light (R) ★ 133
- [ ] Black Like Me   17
- [ ] Black Rider (PG/R) 116
- [ ] Black Spot, The   140
- [ ] Bumps (PG) ★ 126
- [ ] Cattlestar Faticus   12
- [ ] Ciebola (PG) ★★★ 130
- [ ] Ciebola Continuation (X) 130
- [ ] Come and Get It   126
- [ ] Crow's Feet (R) 59
- [ ] Crowd Pleaser   67
- [ ] Cucamonga Honey (R) ★ 74
- [ ] Dragonfly (R) 112
- [ ] Dude, The (R) 73
- [ ] Enemy Within (PG) ★ 18
- [ ] Flintstone (R) ★ 62
- [ ] Forked Tongue (R) ★ 139
- [ ] Frontier Proctologist   150
- [ ] Fuel Rod (PG) ★ 39
- [ ] Get Slick (R) ★ 23
- [ ] Goblin Girl (R) ★ 108
- [ ] Great Escape, The   50
- [ ] Happy Hour (PG/R) ★ 34
- [ ] Hip Boots (R/X) 110
- [ ] Ho Charlie (R/X) 131
- [ ] Inner Vision (R/X) 52
- [ ] Interrogation (R) 73
- [ ] Inverted Staircase (PG/R) ★ 95
- [ ] Kid, The (X) ★ 130
- [ ] Lamb Chops (R/X) 110
- [ ] Lucky Streaks (PG) ★★★ 104
- [ ] Mandric (PG) ★ 20
- [ ] Mother Lode (R) ★ 91
- [ ] Multiplication (R) ★★ 43
- [ ] Nazgul, The   116
- [ ] Old Goats   110
- [ ] Pajama People (PG) ★ 49
- [ ] Prime Cut (PG) ★ 119
- [ ] Quick Stop   69
- [ ] Right   121
- [ ] Run for Cover (R/X) ★★ 107
- [ ] Said and Done   59
- [ ] Serrated Edge (PG) ★★ 115
- [ ] Shit Hooks (R) ★ 44
- [ ] Shot in the Dark (PG/R) ★ 52
- [ ] Silver Slippers   110
- [ ] Skedaddle   67
- [ ] Space Sluts in the Scammer (PG) 51
- [ ] Sting, The (PG) ★★ 29
- [ ] Sunset Prow (PG) ★ 149
- [ ] Sunshine (R) ★★ 112
- [ ] Third Pillar Regular Route (PG/R) ★★★ 87
- [ ] Triology (R) 29
- [ ] Two 4 the Price of One   69
- [ ] Two for the Money   70
- [ ] Unh-Unh   105
- [ ] Voice of the Crags (PG/R) ★ 52
- [ ] Whalin' Dwalin   115
- [ ] Wonderful Wino   97
- [ ] Woodward Finish   129

5.10

- [ ] Bye Spy (R) 151
- [ ] Crag Witch   34
- [ ] Creep Show   151
- [ ] Falkenstein Face (TR) 40
- [ ] Flat Top   25
- [ ] Guardians of the Galaxy (X) 110
- [ ] Half n' Half (R) 151
- [ ] Pussey Paws (R) 121
- [ ] Return Engagement   116
- [ ] Terrorist (X) 117
- [ ] Where the Action Is (PG/R) ★ 75

5.10c

- [ ] 14 Karat (R) ★ 58
- [ ] Achilles (R) 76
- [ ] Aztec Two-Step (R) 92
- [ ] Barely Anything (★PG/R) ★ 24
- [ ] Big Boys Don't Cry (R) ★ 73
- [ ] Buzzers and Hummers 149
- [ ] Can't Say (R) 39
- [ ] Comfortably Numb (R) ★★★ 62
- [ ] Creature from the Black Lagoon (PG) 17
- [ ] Lembert Dome—Direct Northwest Face (PG) ★★★ 73
- [ ] Drinking Buddies (R) 129
- [ ] Drunk n' Horney (PG) 149
- [ ] Ease On It (R) 46
- [ ] Fairest of All (R) 98
- [ ] Fat Boys (PG) ★ 69
- [ ] Fatted Calf (R) ★ 75
- [ ] Fireworks (R) 59
- [ ] Footnote (PG/R) ★ 23
- [ ] Friggin For Higgins (PG) ★ 51
- [ ] Galen's Crack (TR) 40
- [ ] Gizmo 67
- [ ] Gold Standard 43
- [ ] Golden Eagle (R) 83
- [ ] Grass Roots 39
- [ ] Hammered (R/X) 39
- [ ] Here's Johnny (X) ★ 130
- [ ] Hogwash (PG/R) ★ 58
- [ ] Hustler, The 73
- [ ] Inspiration (R/X) ★ 58
- [ ] Karin's Coming 64
- [ ] Kill Pickle (R) 65
- [ ] Knobulator (PG) ★ 62
- [ ] Lakeshore Boulevard (R) ★ 147
- [ ] Lenticular Limbo 87

- [ ] Liberation (R/X) ★ 58
- [ ] Like A Virgin (R) ★ 128
- [ ] Lock of Ages (PG) 18
- [ ] Looking Glass (R) 92
- [ ] Lord of the Overhigh (R) 112
- [ ] Man Over Board (X) ★ 74
- [ ] Olive Oyl (R) 148
- [ ] One Toke Over the Line (R) ★ 130
- [ ] Overhang Over (PG) 15
- [ ] Parable (R) 92
- [ ] Pit Stop 69
- [ ] Plastic Exploding Inevitable 5.10c; A4 (R) 98
- [ ] Playing with a Full Deck (R/X) 128
- [ ] Pressure Vessel (PG) 18
- [ ] Prognosis (PG) ★ 61
- [ ] Shadow of Doubt (PG/R) ★★★ 48
- [ ] Sharks Tooth (PG) 149
- [ ] Spark Plug (PG) ★ 71
- [ ] Stanley Edge, The (PG) 18
- [ ] Step It Up and Go (PG/R) ★ 24
- [ ] Sweet Nothings (R) ★ 24
- [ ] Tastes Great 81
- [ ] Team Yuppy Does Tuolumne (PG) 48
- [ ] Ten A, My Ass 71
- [ ] Thunder Road (PG) ★★ 119
- [ ] Thy Will Be Done (PG) ★ 46
- [ ] Ursula (PG) ★★ 137
- [ ] Vice Gripped. (R) ★ 34
- [ ] Vicious Thing 31
- [ ] Way We Could Have Been ★ 24
- [ ] Whatchacallit 67
- [ ] When You're Strange 105
- [ ] Whipped Cream (PG) ★ 49
- [ ] Who Stole My Flip-Flop 140
- [ ] Yellow Brick Road 68

5.10d

- [ ] Air Play (R) ★ 48
- [ ] Arms Race (PG) ★★★ 113
- [ ] Black and Bluto (R) 148
- [ ] Bulge, The (PG) ★★ 62
- [ ] Chinese Handcuffs (PG) ★ 29
- [ ] Cleared For Take Off (R) 25
- [ ] Daddy's Little Girl (R) ★★ 24
- [ ] Derbyshire 20
- [ ] Double Stuff (R) ★ 74
- [ ] Double Take (PG) 42
- [ ] Ewe Must Be Kidding 110
- [ ] Fairest of Al (PG/R) ★ 97
- [ ] Ferd's Follies 80
- [ ] First Verse (R) 91

- [ ] Four-Finger Slooper (R) 64
- [ ] Fuel Pump (R) 77
- [ ] Geekin' Hard 60
- [ ] General Shortie (X) ★ 130
- [ ] Gimme Some Slack (R) 32
- [ ] Golden Dawn 153
- [ ] Gram Traverse (PG/R) ★★ 112
- [ ] Hemispheres (R) ★ 100
- [ ] Hole in One 147
- [ ] Hooker (R) ★ 25
- [ ] Hurricane Betsy (R/X) ★ 44
- [ ] Hyper Space (R) 128
- [ ] Ice Ten (R) 92
- [ ] Knob Roulette (R/X) 46

──────────────── **5.10d** ────────────────

☐ Knobnoxious (PG) ★★ 62
☐ Knobvious (PG) ★★ 62
☐ Lightweights Don's Scream (R) ★ 73
☐ Lord Caffeine (PG) ★★ 18
☐ Lucky 13 (R) 82
☐ Man's Best Friend 70
☐ Memo from Loyd (PG) ★★ 44
☐ Miss Adventure (R) ★★ 24
☐ Movement in Camouflage (R) ★★ 50
☐ Names in the Guidebook (R) 75
☐ Nutsack (R/X) 92
☐ Old Folks Boogie (kR) ★★ 62
☐ One-Eyed Jack (X) 65
☐ Out of Gas (PG) ★ 137
☐ Oz (PG) ★★★ 112
☐ Party Time 20
☐ Pepe Le Peu 43
☐ Piece of Grass (X) 139
☐ Platapus (PG) ★ 61
☐ Playing with Fire (R) 98

☐ Pop Eye (R) 148
☐ Preface (R) 23
☐ Prince of Pleasure (PG) ★ 24
☐ Pumper (TR) 12
☐ Rabid Right (PG) 149
☐ Razor Back (PG/R) ★★★ 113
☐ Rock Lobster (PG) ★ 29
☐ Rover Take Over (PG) ★★ 62
☐ Scavenger (R) ★★ 103
☐ Second Coming (PG) ★ 127
☐ Sole on Ice (R) 92
☐ Space Rover (R/X) 128
☐ Spectra 64
☐ Table of Contents (R) ★★ 23
☐ Thrill Is Gone, The (PG) ★ 18
☐ Tourist Trap (R) 34
☐ Transformer (PG) ★ 40
☐ Turning Japanese (PG) ★ 25
☐ Two Cams To Open (R) 128
☐ Wages of Sin 70

──────────────── **5.11a** ────────────────

☐ Bikes on Dikes 5.10+ 151
☐ Detective 5.10+ (Rx) 92
☐ Malletosis 5.10+ (R) 24
☐ 15 Seconds of Fame (PG) ★★ 129
☐ Age of Darkness (PG) 18
☐ Air-Cooled Unit (PG) ★ 18
☐ Angelic Upstart (PG/R) ★★ 137
☐ Barbary Coast (R) ★ 48
☐ Bastard from the Bush (R/X) 34
☐ Bearded Clam (PG) ★ 54
☐ Big Gulp 69
☐ Black Angel (PG) ★★★ 21
☐ Block, The Center (R/X) 39
☐ Bushes and Buckets (R) 31
☐ Chvchichǎschtli (PG/R) ★ 57
☐ Compared to What (PG) 41
☐ Cross Reference (R) ★ 23
☐ Cutting Edge, The (R) 73
☐ Detente 64
☐ Fast Track (R) 92
☐ Flapper, The 67
☐ Fluoridation (PG) ★ 20
☐ Foolish Pleasures (PG/R) ★ 24
☐ Friends in High Places 131
☐ Get Into The Groove (PG) ★ 128
☐ Get Sick (PG/R) ★ 44
☐ Goldline 25
☐ Handbook (PG) ★★★ 46
☐ Harpole and the Hendersons (R) ★ 77
☐ Hole in the Wall 81

☐ How Does It Feel? (R) ★ 34
☐ It Is Finished (PG/R) ★ 58
☐ Joystick, The (R/X) 127
☐ Ledge, The (PG/R) ★ 21
☐ Liberal Apologist (PG) 149
☐ Liposuction (PG) ★ 62
☐ Mellow Yellow (R) ★ 77
☐ Mighty Mite 70
☐ Mike and Urmy (PG) ★ 51
☐ Miller Time 151
☐ Moaner (PG/R) 151
☐ No Bones 131
☐ Orange Plasma (PG) ★ 62
☐ Partners in Climb (PG) ★ 65
☐ Pencilitits (PG) ★ 60
☐ Penguin Cafe (PG) ★ 20
☐ Pie in the Sky 51
☐ Pinch A Loaf 20
☐ Plausible Deniability (R) 61
☐ Poodle Boy 68
☐ Pot Luck (TR) 91
☐ Push-Push (PG) ★★ 39
☐ Rapture of the Deep (PG) ★ 149
☐ Resisting Arrest (PG) ★★ 145
☐ Ring Eye, The (PG/R) 151
☐ Rolo Solo (TR) 70
☐ Sausalito Archie's Overhang (R) 29
☐ Shiner (PG) ★ 129
☐ Sixth Nine (PG) ★ 151
☐ Slate Quarry 70

5.11a

- Socerer's Apprentice (R) ★★ 103
- Soft White Underbelly (R) ★★ 138
- Sunstroke 116
- Thigamajic 67
- Tideline (PG) ★★ 18
- Tips Ahoy (R) ★ 58
- Twister 46
- Unnatural Act (R/X) 138

- Virgin Killer (R/X) 131
- Walking the Dog (R) 52
- Whatzisface 67
- White Line Fever (R) 127
- Willie's Hand Jive (R) ★ 74
- Winery, The (R) 129
- Wrinkle in Time (R) ★ 130

5.11b

- Apex Predator (PG/R) ★ 36
- Auto Bond (PG) ★ 20
- Big Time (PG) ★★ 129
- Blackout (X) ★★★ 45
- Body Language ★ 15
- By Hood or By Crook (PG) ★★★ 29
- Cage, The (PG) ★ 16
- Chimbote (R) ★ 147
- Damsel Fly (R) 121
- Decoy (X) 45
- Dirty Dream 34
- Double Eagle (R) ★ 34
- Dynomike (R) 83
- Fort Knox (PG/R) ★★ 139
- Freedom of Choice (PG) ★ 119
- Get to the Roof (R) 82
- Go for the Gold (R) ★ 34
- Golden Bars (PG/R) ★★ 139
- Immaculate Deception (PG) ★ 25
- Inevitable Conclusions (PG/R) ★ 97
- La Bella Luna 105
- Live Wire (R) 18

- Lizard Lips (TR) 20
- Man, A Boy, and His Poodle, A 68
- Math of the Pastor (R/X) 92
- Mr. Kamps (R) ★★ 104
- Night and Day 51
- No Rock Nazis (PG) 29
- One-Armed Bandit ★ 61
- Panning for Nuggets (R) ★ 32
- Paris Is Burning ★ 34
- Pinhead, The (X) ★ 130
- Polski Wyrob (R) ★ 65
- Rat Patrol (PG) 77
- Scorpion (PG) ★★ 122
- Shambles (R) ★ 129
- Speed of Life (PG) ★★★ 86
- Strike It Rich (R/X) 92
- Third World (PG) ★ 29
- Three to Get Ready 70
- Torqued (PG) ★ 82
- Walk Like An Egyptian (PG) ★ 77
- Whip It (X) 119

5.11

- Dazed and Confused 128
- Flash, The (R/X) ★ 50
- Harding Route (PG) ★★★ 84
- Lost in Face (R) 131
- Low Budget 47
- Mesmerized (R) ★ 115

- Obscure Destiny (R) 90
- Prime Chopper, The (R) 25
- Universal Corner (R) 41
- Whozamawhatsit 67
- Workout Man (Tr) 38

5.11c

- Alien (R) ★ 130
- Arch Rival (PG) ★★ 24
- Bachar/Yerian (X) ★★★ 129
- Batteries Not Included ★ 52
- Black & White & Red All Over 68
- Black Magic (R/X) 122
- Blues Riff (PG) ★★★ 41
- Boy and His Dog, A 70
- Burning Down the House (X) ★ 94
- Castoff, The 130
- Coq Au Vin 83
- Corn Hole (R) ★ 31
- Defenders of the Faith (R) 92
- Do or Fly (PG) ★★★ 76
- Double Cream, Double Sugar (PG) ★ 80
- Dreams (PG) ★ 24
- Dress Rehearsal (PG) ★ 129
- Easy Money (PG) ★ 18
- Easy Wind (PG) ★★ 113
- Executive Decision (R) ★ 80
- Exposé (R/X) 98
- Follow Your Heart (R/X) 128
- Full House 128
- Full Speed Ahead 86
- Grand Slam 71
- Ground Effects (PG) ★★ 110
- Guy Takes A Bomma Gutsa 129
- Into The Void (PG/R) ★★ 54
- Jawbone Jitterbug 82
- Jiffy Pop (PG) ★★ 69
- Johnny Rock (R/X) ★ 47
- Knuckle Ball 126
- Le Papillon (PG) ★★ 69
- Less Filling (PG) ★ 81
- Live To Tell (R) 128
- Made for the Shade (R) 82
- Material World (PG) ★ 128
- Midnight Hour (PG) 53
- Missing Link (PG) ★★ 113
- Motor Home for Midgets 47
- Omega Race (PG/R) ★ 123
- Paiste Formula (PG) ★★ 34
- Perspiration (PG/R) ★ 58
- Pièce de Résistance (R) ★★ 101
- Pirouette Roof (R) ★ 138
- Pygmy Variation (PG) 48
- Roadkill (PG) ★ 42
- Shell Shock (PG) ★ 129
- Slipstream (PG/R) ★ 123
- Solstice (R) 17
- Sometimes A Great Notion (TR) 20
- Steep Thrills (R) 44
- Suicide Solution (X) ★ 119
- Susie Q (PG) ★ 68
- Swiss Orange Chip (R/X) 130
- Tin Pan Alley (R) ★ 48
- Titslinger (R) ★ 82
- Torque Yer Mudda (PG) ★ 51
- Vapor Lock (PG) ★ 123
- Wienie Roast (R) ★ 56

5.11d

- Bag 'o Tricks (PG) ★★ 83
- Cat Spray (PG/R) 129
- Centinella (R) ★ 131
- Death Crack (PG) ★★★ 21
- Diagnosis (PG) ★ 61
- Dik Me A Dog (R) 127
- Double Feature (PG) ★ 18
- Fairwell to Kings, A (R) ★ 96
- Fierce Tiger on Rock (R) 147
- Gettin' in the Groove (PG) ★ 20
- Groundout (R/X) ★ 34
- Hot Box (PG) ★ 18
- Hysteria (PG) ★★★ 113
- Itchy Scratchy (PG) ★★ 77
- Just What The Doctor Ordered 17
- Lead Doll (PG) ★ 129
- Lone Ranger (PG) ★ 128
- Meltdown, The (X) ★★ 141
- Mr. Toad's Wild Ride (R) ★★ 102
- Murder by Numbers (R) ★ 48
- Never Give Up the Ship (R/X) 74
- Ornithology (PG) ★★ 16
- Pilot's License (R/X) 127
- Poindexter (PG) ★★ 83
- Priaprism (PG/R) ★ 128
- Public Enemy (PG) ★ 39
- Realm of the Absurd (R) ★ 34
- Scratch 'n Sniff (PG) ★★ 77
- Skeletor (R) ★ 48
- Slider-Banger (R) ★★ 129
- Soul Power (PG) ★★ 149
- SS, The (R/X) 127
- Start Bouldering (X) ★ 45
- Sunny Side Down (R) 56
- Trickanosis (PG) ★ 61
- Wailing Wall (PG) ★★★ 122

5.12a

- ☐ Bruce Proof Roof 5.11+   59
- ☐ Swinger 5.11+ (R/X) ★ 130
- ☐ Virgin Testimony 5.11+ (R) 131
- ☐ Angel Eyes (PG) ★ 44
- ☐ Beyond A Shadow of Doubt (R) ★ 47
- ☐ Blue Moon (PG) ★★ 71
- ☐ Body Count (PG) ★★ 45
- ☐ Claim Jumper   137
- ☐ Codex   87
- ☐ Cole Burner (R) 69
- ☐ Countdown (X) ★ 45
- ☐ Coup de Gras (R/X) 102
- ☐ Cupcake (PG) ★★★ 68
- ☐ Deviate, The (PG) 46
- ☐ Devil Dog (PG) ★ 41
- ☐ Dinky Doink (R) ★ 151
- ☐ EZ Duz It (PG) ★★★ 85
- ☐ Feral Waife   21
- ☐ Foott Route (R) ★ 139
- ☐ Go With The Flow (PG) ★ 65
- ☐ Gold Finger (PG) ★★★ 41
- ☐ Golden Years   34
- ☐ Grace Under Pressure (R/X) ★★ 25
- ☐ Heart of Stone (R) ★★ 102
- ☐ Heinous   138
- ☐ Horseshoes and Handgrenades (PG)
       ★★★ 76
- ☐ Ivory Tower Body-Double (PG) 18
- ☐ King of the Hill   129
- ☐ Living in Sin   129
- ☐ Lord of the Apes (PG) ★ 152
- ☐ Mean Left (R) ★ 83
- ☐ Neurosis (PG) ★ 61
- ☐ Osmosis (PG) ★ 61
- ☐ Precious Bodily Fluids (TR) 20
- ☐ Quantum Leap (PG) ★ 65
- ☐ Quick Sand (PG) ★★ 149
- ☐ Radar Detector   80
- ☐ Reanimator (R) 18
- ☐ Reptilian Brain Syndrome (R) 54
- ☐ Royal Flush (PG) ★★ 128
- ☐ Shipoopi! (PG/R) ★★★ 129
- ☐ Slim Pickins (R) 131
- ☐ Spellbound   128
- ☐ Spiro Gyro (PG) ★ 65
- ☐ Stones Throw (PG) ★★ 83
- ☐ Straight Away ★★ 71
- ☐ Testify (PG) ★ 116
- ☐ Top Pickle (PG/R) ★ 65
- ☐ Ugle Arête (PG) ★ 42
- ☐ Wicked Itchy (R) ★★ 77
- ☐ Wicked Shortie (PG) ★★ 84
- ☐ Wild Streak (PG) ★ 48

5.12b

- ☐ Carcass (PG) 42
- ☐ Dough Boy (PG) ★ 68
- ☐ Engine in Distress ★ 41
- ☐ Felix (PG) ★★ 83
- ☐ Heat Sensitive (PG) ★ 29
- ☐ High Heels (PG) ★★★ 39
- ☐ Icing (PG) ★★★ 68
- ☐ Iya (PG) ★★ 82
- ☐ Lighter Side (PG) ★★★ 122
- ☐ Master Cylinder (PG) ★★★ 83
- ☐ Power of Soul (PG) ★★ 149
- ☐ Quick Release (PG) ★★ 42
- ☐ Realitivity (PG) ★ 65
- ☐ Rebel Yell (PG) ★★ 53
- ☐ Red Don't Go (PG) ★★ 77
- ☐ Shut It Up (PG) ★ 50
- ☐ Silver Bullet (PG) ★★★ 83
- ☐ Stubble Face   113
- ☐ We Want EZ (PG) ★★★ 85
- ☐ Wicked Stiffy (PG) ★★ 77

5.12

- ☐ Boa (R/X) ★ 138
- ☐ Body and Soul (X) ★★★ 45
- ☐ Cheat Stone (X) ★★★ 45

5.12c

- [ ] Black Dahlia   129
- [ ] Bombs Over Tokyo   56
- [ ] Cowabunga (PG) ★★ 54
- [ ] Dangle Fest (PG) ★★ 82
- [ ] Earshot   82
- [ ] Electric Africa (PG) ★★★ 141
- [ ] Finger, The (PG) ★★ 83
- [ ] Grenade Launcher (PG) ★★★ 76
- [ ] Lover Not A Fighter   140
- [ ] Party Bowl (PG) ★ 69

- [ ] Patticake (PG) ★ 68
- [ ] Pretty in Pink Point (PG) ★ 129
- [ ] Schneiderato, The (R/X) 127
- [ ] Shadow Warriors (PG) ★★★ 45
- [ ] Show Don't Tell   126
- [ ] Spike (PG) ★★ 82
- [ ] Syncronicity (PG) ★ 65
- [ ] Truth or Dare (PG) ★★ 129 Xtra (R) ★★ 82
- [ ] Xtra (R) ★★ 84

5.12d

- [ ] Cruise Control (PG) ★★ 110
- [ ] Fame and Fortune (PG) ★★ 45
- [ ] Ice (PG) ★★ 112
- [ ] Lazer Blade (PG) ★★ 42
- [ ] Mystery Achievement (PG/R) ★ 48

- [ ] Perhaps, Another Bowl? (PG) ★★★ 69
- [ ] Positivity (PG) ★★ 53
- [ ] Rap It Up (R) ★★ 48
- [ ] Skin Walker (PG) ★★ 141

5.13a

- [ ] Love Supreme 5.13 (PG) ★★ 42
- [ ] Bandaloop (PG) ★★★ 129
- [ ] Clash of the Titans (PG) ★★ 141
- [ ] Grapevine (PG) ★★★ 65

- [ ] Helter Skelter   24
- [ ] Medusa (PG) ★ 141
- [ ] Sudden Impact (PG) ★ 65
- [ ] Whippersnapper (PG) ★★ 145

5.13b

- [ ] Bogey Meets Mr. Porcupine (PG) ★ 129
- [ ] Circus-Circus (PG) ★★ 129

- [ ] European Vacation (PG) ★★ 141
- [ ] Love Sexy (PG) ★★ 45
- [ ] Super Sonic (PG) ★★ 45

5.13c

- [ ] Raging Waters (PG) ★ 129

- [ ] Rising Sun (PG) ★★★ 141

INDEX

Access: It's everybody's concern

the ACCESS FUND

THE ACCESS FUND, a national, non-profit climbers organization, is working to keep you climbing. The Access Fund helps preserve access and protect the environment by providing funds for land acquisitions and climber support facilities, financing scientific studies, publishing educational materials promoting low-impact climbing, and providing start-up money, legal counsel and other resources to local climbers' coalitions.

Climbers can help preserve access by being responsible users of climbing areas. Here are some practical ways to support climbing:

- **COMMIT YOURSELF TO "LEAVING NO TRACE."** Pick up litter around campgrounds and the crags. Let your actions inspire others.

- **DISPOSE OF HUMAN WASTE PROPERLY.** Use toilets whenever possible. If none are available, choose a spot at least 50 meters from any water source. Dig at hole 6 inches (15 cm) deep, and bury your waste in it. *Always pack out toilet paper* in a "Zip-Lock"-type bag.

- **UTILIZE EXISTING TRAILS.** Avoid cutting switchbacks and trampling vegetation.

- **USE DISCRETION WHEN PLACING BOLTS AND OTHER "FIXED" PROTECTION.** Camouflage all anchors with rock-colored paint. Use chains for rappel stations, or leave rock-colored webbing.

- **RESPECT RESTRICTIONS THAT PROTECT NATURAL RESOURCES AND CULTURAL ARTIFACTS .** Appropriate restrictions can include prohibition of climbing around Indian rock art, pioneer inscriptions, and on certain formations during raptor nesting season. Power drills are illegal in wilderness areas. *Never chisel or sculpt holds in rock on public lands, uless it is expressly allowed* – no other practice so seriously threatens our sport.

- **PARK IN DESIGNATED AREAS,** not in undevelpoed, vegetated areas. Carpool to the crags!

- **MAINTAIN A LOW PROFILE.** Other people have the same right to undisturbed enjoyment of natural areas as do you.

- **RESPECT PRIVATE PROPERTY.** Don't trespass in order to climb.

- **JOIN OR FORM A GROUP TO DEAL WITH ACCESS ISSUES IN YOUR AREA.** Consider clean-ups, trail building or maintenance, or other "goodwill" projects.

- **JOIN THE ACCESS FUND.** To become a member, *simply make a donation (tax-deductible) of any amount.* Only by working together can we preserve the diverse American climbing experience.

The Access Fund. Preserving America's diverse climbing resources.
The Access Fund • P.O. Box 17010 • Boulder, CO 80308